# Cambridge Elements

Elements in Soviet and Post-Soviet History
edited by
Mark Edele
*University of Melbourne*
Rebecca Friedman
*Florida International University*

# ENVIRONMENT AND SOCIETY IN SOVIET ESTONIA, 1960–1990

*An Intimate Cultural History*

Epp Annus
*Tallinn University and
Ohio State University*

## CAMBRIDGE
UNIVERSITY PRESS

Shaftesbury Road, Cambridge CB2 8EA, United Kingdom

One Liberty Plaza, 20th Floor, New York, NY 10006, USA

477 Williamstown Road, Port Melbourne, VIC 3207, Australia

314–321, 3rd Floor, Plot 3, Splendor Forum, Jasola District Centre, New Delhi – 110025, India

103 Penang Road, #05–06/07, Visioncrest Commercial, Singapore 238467

Cambridge University Press is part of Cambridge University Press & Assessment, a department of the University of Cambridge.

We share the University's mission to contribute to society through the pursuit of education, learning and research at the highest international levels of excellence.

www.cambridge.org
Information on this title: www.cambridge.org/9781009429351

DOI: 10.1017/9781009429368

© Epp Annus 2025

This work is in copyright. It is subject to statutory exceptions and to the provisions of relevant licensing agreements; with the exception of the Creative Commons version the link for which is provided below, no reproduction of any part of this work may take place without the written permission of Cambridge University Press.

An online version of this work is published at doi.org/10.1017/9781009429368 under a Creative Commons Open Access licence CC-BY-NC-ND 4.0 which permits re-use, distribution and reproduction in any medium for non-commercial purposes providing appropriate credit to the original work is given. You may not distribute derivative works without permission. To view a copy of this licence, visit Deed – Attribution-NonCommercial-NoDerivatives 4.0 International – Creative Commons.

All versions of this work may contain content reproduced under license from third parties. Permission to reproduce this third-party content must be obtained from these third-parties directly.

When citing this work, please include a reference to the DOI 10.1017/9781009429368

First published 2025

*A catalogue record for this publication is available from the British Library*

ISBN 978-1-009-53948-7 Hardback
ISBN 978-1-009-42935-1 Paperback
ISSN 2753-5290 (online)
ISSN 2753-5282 (print)

Cambridge University Press & Assessment has no responsibility for the persistence or accuracy of URLs for external or third-party internet websites referred to in this publication and does not guarantee that any content on such websites is, or will remain, accurate or appropriate.

# Environment and Society in Soviet Estonia, 1960–1990

## An Intimate Cultural History

Elements in Soviet and Post-Soviet History

DOI: 10.1017/9781009429368
First published online: October 2025

---

Epp Annus
*Tallinn University and
Ohio State University*
Author for correspondence: Epp Annus, annus.1@osu.edu

**Abstract:** Russia's twenty-first-century military aggression has inspired calls for rethinking the Soviet era and its aftermath – for drawing attention to decolonizing efforts within the (former) USSR and to Russia's colonial practices and imperial aspirations. At the same time, the present era of anthropogenic climate change urges us to consider the global and planetary implications of local actions. This Element combines these two scholarly impulses to consider Soviet-era Estonian society between the 1960s and the 1980s: it investigates how natural environments and social ideas and circumstances were intertwined in fundamental ways, and it emphasizes local agency over homogenizing strategies of Soviet rule. Estonians cared deeply about their local environments, but they also took inspiration from environmentalist works of global importance. Various aspects of Estonian environmental thought and practice are analyzed as tied to local, intimate environments, as impacted by Soviet/Russian colonial rule, and as connected to the global circulation of ideas. This title is also available as open access on Cambridge Core.

**Keywords:** Estonian SSR, environmental studies, Soviet Union, multiscalarity, decolonization

© Epp Annus 2025

ISBNs: 9781009539487 (HB), 9781009429351 (PB), 9781009429368 (OC)
ISSNs: 2753-5290 (online), 2753-5282 (print)

# Contents

Introduction — 1

1 *Reverence for Life*: Bridging Local and Global Environmental Perspectives. 1965 — 5

2 The Forbidden Sea and Colonial Violence. 1976 — 26

3 *The Sound of the Choir Is the Sound of the Earth*: The Song, the Land, the Nation, and Decolonization. 1969, 1869, 1988 — 43

4 Urbanitis and Limits to Growth. 1978 — 66

Conclusion. Thirty Years Later: Bound to Nature in a Digital Society — 80

## Introduction

*Estonia. A small country situated on the shores of the Baltic Sea, with over 2,200 islands and islets (see Figure 1). Over half its territory is covered by forests. Population about 1.4 million. Member state of the European Union and NATO since 2004. Highly advanced in digital technologies, well-secured e-voting in use since 2005. A democratic state. Among the least corrupt countries in the world.*

*Independent republic 1918–1940; then forcibly annexed into the Soviet Union. After three years of German occupation during World War II, it was, in 1944, re-annexed by the USSR. Independent statehood was regained in 1991.*

*Population changes in the Soviet era: in 1935, ethnic Estonians composed 88.1 percent of the total population; in 1945, after Hitler's* Umsiedlung, *the proportion was 97.3 percent; by 1989, ethnic Estonians composed 61.5 percent of the total.*

*First nature reserve: 1910, a bird sanctuary on the Vaikla islets. First nature conservation law: 1935. First national park: 1971.*

*Estonian language: a Finnic language of the Uralic language family; closest to Finnish, but also related to Livonian, Votic, and Ingrian languages.*

Soon, four decades will have passed since 1986, when processes of decolonization started within the Soviet Union. On the Baltic shores, full Soviet/Russian colonial-style control lasted, similarly, about forty years. In Estonia, Soviet rule was fully established only by 1949, when the deportations of about 200,000 people from Estonia, Latvia, and Lithuania destroyed the support base for organized resistance. Thirty-nine years later, in 1988, the Estonian Sovereignty Declaration asserted the supremacy of Estonian laws over those of Moscow's central rule.

This Element focuses on society and the environment in Soviet Estonia within a limited frame of thirty years, 1960–1990 – but it also tells a story of continuities across times and places. It follows the flow of ideas across continents, as well as the continuing life of earlier histories within the ever-unfolding course of social time.

In its investigations of spatial and temporal continuities, one central claim of this Element is that the Soviet Union was not always, in all its localities, and in all its aspects, so thoroughly Soviet. Sovietness – that is, value-systems, beliefs, and practices imposed by Soviet/Russian rule upon both ordinary people and cultural elites – was not necessarily the defining category in everyday life or in the circulation of ideas. While authoritarian colonial control delimited the boundaries of the possible for Estonians and others, within these boundaries there was nevertheless room for a range of thought and action – moreover, through the years, the limits of the possible were constantly contested and sometimes extended.[1]

---

[1] Epp Annus, *Soviet Postcolonial Studies: A View from the Western Borderlands* (New York: Routledge, 2018).

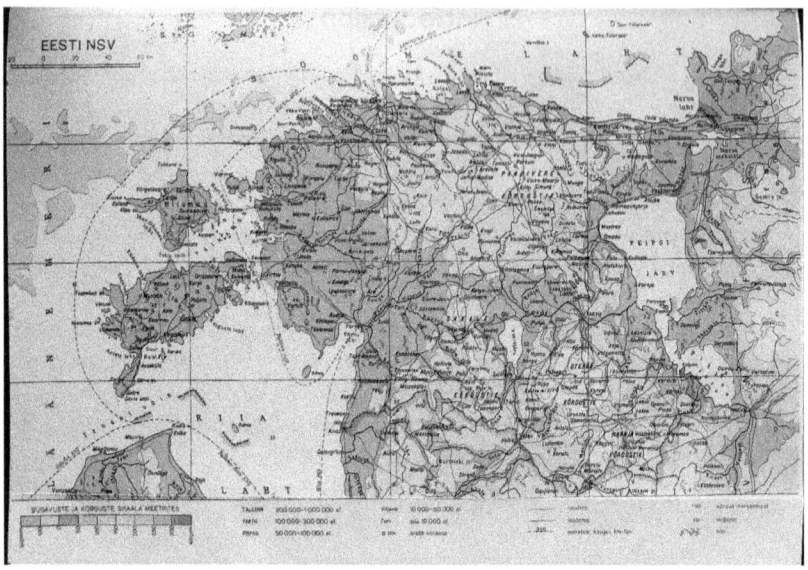

**Figure 1** A geographic map of the Estonian SSR. 1978.
**Source**: Nõukogude Eesti. Tallinn: Valgus.

In the Baltics regions, people's thoughts, values, and everyday practices continued to include ideas, values, and beliefs inherited from their pre-Soviet past. These became jumbled together with the newly imposed official ideology and a large variety of ideas and imaginaries from cultural zones beyond the Soviet Union. And living memory of the pre-Soviet past very much persisted through the Soviet decades: Lennart Meri, for example, was born in independent Estonia in 1929, went to school in Germany and France, was deported to Siberia in 1941, became a well-known author and filmmaker in the 1970s and the president of the Estonian Republic from 1992 to 2001. My great-aunt Ella was born in 1903 and died in 1990 – and, for the whole of my childhood, her years of retirement, she showed little restraint in expressing her hatred for Russian rule. Russian rule – this was how the new rule, imposed through strategies of systemic violence by a Russia-dominated colonial matrix of power, was commonly referred to in everyday parlance.

Even as annexed into the Soviet Union, Estonians – like other nations within the USSR – were not altogether cut off from ideas circulating in the rest of the world. This Element traces Estonian responses to Albert Schweitzer's ethics of a *Reverence for life*, to Rachel Carson's book *Silent Spring*, to the Club of Rome report *Limits to Growth*, and it follows how Estonian discussions about nature and the environment often presented these themes as simultaneously local, regional, and global. One way to understand this era, I propose, is through a multiscalar approach, which does not privilege Soviet ideology as the single most determinative constituent of the era, but which follows how personal, regional, national, global, and planetary concerns all played their role.[2]

Indeed especially from the mid-1960s onward, the connections and intertwinings of personal experiences with local and global concerns emerge clearly in Estonian society. A truly ethical worldview, Estonian intellectuals would repeatedly stress after Schweitzer, can only be based on an "ethical sense for one's unity with all of nature."[3] This ethical stance was figured as proceeding from an intimate connection with one's immediate surroundings, from sensations of awe and wonder while walking in the woods, swimming in the sea, or sitting on the doorstep of an old farmhouse – and, from that primary connection, coming to acknowledge a shared global responsibility for shared global challenges (see Section 1).

Pre-Soviet conceptions of nature, legacies of environmental advocacy, and an array of cultural traditions continued to play a role in Soviet-era Estonia. Although almost anything related to independent statehood during the interwar period was censored with the utmost rigor, the nineteenth-century Baltic-German era, a common past for both Estonia and Latvia under the Russian Empire, was given significant attention in the 1970s and 1980s. The Baltic governorates, an era of a double Baltic-German and Russian colonial rule, had been instrumental in the development of Estonian and Latvian national cultures: tellingly, before the Russification wave of the 1880s, the Germanization of the educated classes was seen as a fundamental threat to Estonians' and Latvians' nascent efforts in nation-building. Moreover, Baltic German culture and Baltic German intellectuals – Johann Gottfried Herder in Riga, Karl Ernst von Baer, Gustav Helmersen, Jakob von Uexküll and others in Estonia – all made lasting contributions both to local cultural developments and to the figuration of local natural environments (see Sections 1 and 3).

The central focus of this Element is naturecultural coexistence, that is, how nature and culture, plants and rocks and seas, and all living species, are involved in shaping human histories, and how human thought and action has engaged with all living things. Since the early 2000s, the term "natureculture" has been widely used to denote the thoroughgoing connectedness of "nature" and "culture,"[4] to highlight the artificiality of the nature-culture opposition, and to overcome the prevailing neglect of anything nonhuman in thinking about

---

[2] Epp Annus, "Multiscalar Decolonization: Estonia's Transition from the Early 1980s to the 1990s," in *Aesthetic Democracy and the Collapse of Soviet Rule: Transformations in Estonian Culture in the 1980s and 1990s*, eds. Virve Sarapik, Epp Annus, Neeme Lopp (under review).

[3] Ain Raitviir, "Aukartus elu ees," *Looming*, no. 12 (1970): 1867.

[4] Donna Haraway, *The Companion Species Manifesto: Dogs, People, and Significant Otherness* (Chicago: Prickly Paradigm Press, 2003).

society and history. In the Estonian context, instead of positing an ideal of virgin "wilderness" untouched by human activity, the environment figured by cultural narratives between the 1960s and the 1980s appeared specifically as created and sustained within a co-existence of human, animal, plant, and soil. The wooded meadow (*puisniit*), for example, of "sparse natural stands with an annually mown herb layer," something still found in parts of Estonia, has supported a biodiversity superior to both forests and natural meadowlands.[5] When Lahemaa National Park, the first national park in the USSR, was created in 1971 to include forests and swamps, farm lands and Baltic German manor houses, it was this mixed landscape with the strong presence of cultural history that was considered valuable and in need of preservation.

This Element can thus be read as a short history of nature-related ideas, values, and images of cultural significance in one small corner of the USSR. The term "cultural imaginaries," one of the central concepts organizing the following pages, conveys this cluster most precisely. The sea, erratic boulders, pre-industrial landscapes with small farms set amid hill and forestland, the forests themselves, the towers of medieval Tallinn, the pillars of the University of Tartu – culture tells its evolving story through a combination of ideas, values, and images. Sounds, too, are part of this history: choral song, the rustling of wind, the rumble of waves. Tradition, cultural memory, and the personal, affective relationship one sustains to concrete surroundings – all play a role here.[6]

This Element, then, is interested in the plurality of a living culture. It traces coexisting strands in the Estonian conception of nature: one oriented toward environmentalist advocacy, urging people to defend their local environments (Section 1), another turning to intimate nature-experiences to seek one's "true self" (Section 2), a third critiquing virgin-lands campaigns and destructive Soviet-era agricultural technologies (Section 1), a fourth connecting to global environmental movements (Sections 1, 4), a fifth building national identity through songs about the land and sea (Section 3), a sixth standing against colonial extractivism and restrictions on personal movement (Sections 2–3), a seventh expressing fears for the extinction of the human species (Section 4), an eighth seeking authenticity in Finno-Ugric traditions (Section 3), a ninth exploring alienation, global processes of urbanization, and displaying ambivalent attitudes toward natural environments (Section 4). The aim is to reveal

---

[5] Kalevi Kull, Toomas Kukk, and Aleksei Lotman, "When Culture Supports Biodiversity: The Case of the Wooded Meadow," in *Imagining Nature: Practices of Cosmology and Identity*, ed. Andreas Roepstorff, Nils Bubandt, and Kalevi Kul (Aarhus: Aarhus University Press, 2003), 78.

[6] Epp Annus, "Estonians' European Imaginaries: The Soviet and Pre-Soviet Legacy," in *European Constitutionalism the Other Way Round: From the Periphery to the Centre*, ed. Jan Komárek, Birgit Aasa, Marina Bán and Michał Krajewski (Cambridge: Cambridge University Press, forthcoming).

multiple views and voices, dig out their convergences, and attend to their differences. To further extend the theme of continuities, each section ends with a brief essayistic excursion into the present era.

## 1 *Reverence for Life*: Bridging Local and Global Environmental Perspectives. 1965

On September 19, 1965, the daily newspaper *Edasi* published an essay titled *Albert Schweitzer*, written by Ain Kaalep, an Estonian poet and freelance translator, a man familiar with the art of good storytelling. Kaalep begins his piece in a novelistic mode:

> On a spring morning sixty-nine years ago, a young theology student in Alsace, which at that time belonged to the German Empire, came to the thought that his life so far had been very fortunate. So fortunate indeed that he felt compelled to repay his debt. So he decided to dedicate his mature years to active human love.[7]

Kaalep then writes of Schweitzer's extraordinary decision to leave behind a highly successful career as a scholar and musician and instead study medicine with the aim of becoming a doctor.

Thus Albert Schweitzer came to finance and establish a hospital in Lambaréné, French Equatorial Africa, where he worked until his death in September 1965.[8] His commitment to "active human love" involved him in the international peace movement – which earned him a Nobel Peace Prize in 1953 – and in the development of an ethical vision of the interconnectedness of all living beings, an articulation that inspired millions around the globe. Schweitzer's death two weeks earlier is a fact that Kaalep's essay mentions only in passing.

Kaalep's essay instead offers a series of quotes by Schweitzer, including what were perhaps Schweitzer's most cited lines:

> At sunset on the third day, at the very moment when we were making our way through a herd of hippopotamuses, there flashed upon my mind, unforeseen and unsought, the phrase *Reverence for Life*. The iron door had at last given way: a pathway through the thicket had become visible. I had found my way to the principle in which affirmation of the world and ethics are joined together.[9]

---

[7] Ain Kaalep, "Albert Schweitzer," *Edasi*, September 19, 1965. TASS had already released a brief notice of Schweitzer's death, e.g. "Suri Albert Schweitzer," *Edasi*, September 7, 1965. TASS (Telegrafnoye agentstvo Sovetskogo Soyuza) was the official news agency of the Soviet Union.

[8] Schweitzer first gained international renown as one of the most celebrated organists and Bach-interpreters of his day. Schweitzer's vision was constrained by the horizons of his era, the mid-twentieth century: he was fiercely anticolonial, yet he could be paternalistic toward the natives at his hospital in Lambaréné; he was deeply influenced by Indian religions, yet his readings will strike contemporary eyes as Orientalist.

[9] Kaalep, "Albert Schweitzer."

Environmental thought between the 1960s and the 1980s took inspiration from a diverse body of thinkers, but the work of Albert Schweitzer (1875–1965) made an especially distinguished contribution to the Estonian scene. Following Schweitzer's death in 1965, discussions of Schweitzer's ethical thinking began to appear in the Estonian media: in January 1966, in the daily *Noorte Hääl*, Eerik Kumari, chairman of the Nature Protection Committee of the Academy of Sciences of the ESSR, explained how technical progress brings about the deterioration of living environments for humans, animals, and plants. His article, titled *To Defend Life*, foregrounded Schweitzer's "reverence for life" as one of the keywords for the modern conservation of life.[10] Two years later, in May 1968, on the front page of the daily newspaper *Edasi*, Kumari's article *Aukartus elu ees* [*Reverence for Life*] proposes "ten commandments for the protection of nature": Kumari starts the list with clean air and clean water, and concludes it with reverence for life.[11] In 1969, in the journal *Nõukogude Kool* [*Soviet School*], Jaan Eilart, a prominent environmental activist, suggested supplementing school curricula with concrete pedagogical steps based on Schweitzer's ideas: these steps would include promoting the general aim of "sustaining and developing maximum ecological diversity" as the main task "everywhere on Earth, on all continents, in all locations."[12] In 1970, in a lengthy essay about Schweitzer's life and thoughts, entitled – again – *Aukartus elu ees* [*Reverence for life*], Ain Raitviir explains: "According to Schweitzer, an ethical system concerned only with human beings and society cannot provide a harmonious worldview." Raitviir goes on to elaborate how "an ethical worldview is actually an ethical sense for one's unity with all of nature."[13] In 1985, Kalevi Kull's and Rein Kuresoo's detailed review article gives an overview of Estonian Schweitzeriana, asserting Schweitzer's role in establishing "a potential foundation to modern ecological ethics."[14] By that time, two book-length translations of Schweitzer's writings had been issued,[15] a biography had been published,[16] and, in Vanemuine theatre, a play by Osvald Tooming on the life of Schweitzer was staged to great success.[17]

---

[10] Eerik Kumari, "Kaitsta elu," Noorte Hääl, January 29, 1966.
[11] Eerik Kumari, "Aukartus elu ees," Edasi, May 12, 1968.
[12] Jaan Eilart, "Teoreetilisi lähtekohti looduskaitse käsitlemiseks koolis," *Nõukogude Kool*, no. 7 (1969): 538, 541.
[13] Ain Raitviir, "Aukartus elu ees," *Looming*, no. 12 (1970): 1867.
[14] Kalevi Kull and Rein Kuresoo, "Albert Schweitzer Eestis," *Looming*, no. 7 (1985): 989.
[15] An Estonian collection of Schweitzer's essays *Aukartus elu ees* [Reverence for Life] was published in 1972, and *Kultuur ja eetika* followed in 1984. In Latvian, *Vēstules no Lambarenes* (Letters from Lambaréné) was published in 1982, in Lithuanian, *Tarp vandenų ir džiunglių* (Between Water and Jungle) in 1979; *Kultūra ir etika* in 1989.
[16] A lengthy and detailed biography *Schweitzer*, written by Boris Nosik (1971), was translated from Russian into Estonian (1976) and Latvian (1980).
[17] Peeter Tulviste, "Albert Schweitzer 'Vanemuise' laval," *Sirp ja Vasar*, March 20, 1981.

What in particular was so extraordinary about the life and thoughts of this man, such that his impact spread so readily across languages and cultures? Why would the biologist Maie Valt make reference to Schweitzer in her monograph about Karl Ernst von Baer, who lived a century earlier?[18] Why would the newspaper *Noorte Hääl* publish a tale on New Year's Day, 1977, in which two friends explain Albert Schweitzer to *näärivana* (a Sovietised Santa Claus)?[19] Like Gandhi, Schweitzer lived what he wrote; his plain commitment to serving others gave his written word a special force and authority. From his deeply sensed connection with the world around him, there developed, as if quite naturally, an active position of ecological ethics. His accessible style made it easy for readers to understand his call for a "boundlessly expanded responsibility for all living beings," a responsibility shared by all individuals in a very concrete and direct way.[20]

Schweitzer's aforementioned quote, appearing in Kaalep's essay, offers a beautiful image of how his thought developed out of his encounters with the living world: at sunset, in the midst of a herd of hippopotamuses, an understanding arrives that becomes central to his writing: reverence for life. Such a simple idea was easy to embrace. As the Estonian poet Jaan Kaplinski has suggested, Schweitzer articulated what many had already felt and sensed: the enchantment and the beauty of the living world and the need to protect and preserve it.[21] With the support of Schweitzer's cultural prestige, such position could be declared as a foundation for an ethical life. Thus, Schweitzer's ideas helped readers take feelings of concern about local and global environmental devastations and transform them into an ecological worldview with an ethical stance.

## Growing Environmental Awareness in 1960s Estonia

And the time was ripe: Schweitzer's death came at a moment in which environmental awareness was on the rise in Estonia, as in many other parts of the world. Even as the Estonian social order had undergone a near total restructuring after the Soviet annexation, a significant cultural continuity was nonetheless sustained: of prewar environmental initiatives, the Estonian Society for Nature Research, founded in 1853, had continued its activities, albeit now as a division of the Academy of Sciences of the Estonian SSR. Jaan Eilart (born 1933), one of the major figures of the Estonian environmental movement between the 1960s

---

[18] Maie Valt, K. E. v. Baer ja darvinism: Etüüd arenguideede draamast bioloogias (Tallinn: Valgus, 1977), 11–12.
[19] Juhan Aare, "Elagu elu! Näärimuinasjutt," *Noorte Hääl*, January 1, 1977.
[20] Albert Schweitzer, *Kultuur ja eetika*, trans. Mati Sirkel (Tallinn: Eesti Raamat, 1984), 267.
[21] Jaan Kaplinski, "Ökoloogia ja ökonoomika," in See ja teine (Tallinn: Eesti Digiraamatute Keskus, 2013), 53–54.

and the 1980s, had joined as an affiliated member in 1950 and as a full member in 1953. Eilart's activities there included already much of what he undertook later: fieldwork, organizing youth, and writing popular articles.[22]

After the death of Joseph Stalin in 1953, the 1950s saw a notable increase in officially sanctioned environmental activities. In 1955, the Commission on the Protection of Nature started its work within the all-Union Academy of Sciences; following this, the same year, the Nature Conservation Commission of the Academy of Sciences of the Estonian SSR was established, with the young Jaan Eilart as its secretary and Eerik Kumari as its long-serving head. In 1957, a law of pivotal importance was adopted to promote the conservation of nature – the first republic-level conservation law in the Soviet Union, and the first Soviet-era nature reserves in Estonia were created in Vaika, Viidumäe, Matsalu, and Nigula. In Douglas Weiner's summation, "Estonian law led the way for the entire USSR."[23]

In 1958, Jaan Eilart began teaching nature conservation at the University of Tartu, and that same year he founded the Tartu Students' Nature Conservation Circle, the first student society for nature conservation in the USSR and perhaps the first in the world. The same year, the journal "Eesti Loodus" (*Estonian Nature*) was re-launched and became a highly popular publication – notwithstanding its steadily growing print runs, new issues disappeared from kiosks within hours and the fixed number of issues available for pre-order was insufficient to meet popular demand.[24]

In 1966, the Nature Conservation Society of the Estonian SSR was established and swiftly became a truly mass organization; by the mid-1980s, it had approximately 22,000 members. By the 1960s, graduates of the Tartu Nature Conservation Circle were dispersed all over Estonia, and could contribute locally to the launch of activities by the Nature Conservation Society.[25] One of the many achievements of the society was the establishment of Lahemaa National Park in 1971, the first national park in the Soviet Union.[26]

---

[22] National Archives of Estonia, EAA.5311.22/57.41.

[23] Douglas R. Weiner, *A Little Corner of Freedom: Russian Nature Protection from Stalin to Gorbachev* (Berkeley: University of California Press, 1999), 258.

[24] Growing print runs and high demand were routinely discussed at the board meetings of *Eesti Loodus*. It was greatly irritating for the editors that the journal produced good profits, but was not allowed to use these to raise the rather meagre honoraria of its authors. *Toimetuse koosolekute protokollid*, EAA.5306.1.45; EAA.5306.1.31; EAA.5306.1.17.

[25] "Pool sajandit looduskaitserajal. Eesti Looduskaitse Seltsi asutajaliiget, geograaf Jaan Remmelit küsitlenud Ann Marvet," *Eesti Loodus*, no. 10 (2006): 34.

[26] Robert W. Smurr, "Lahemaa: The Paradox of the USSR's First National Park," *Nationalities Papers* 36, no. 3 (2008): 399–423. Latvians soon followed suit and Gauja National Park was established in 1973.

If the late 1960s were marked by history as the era of the Prague Spring and the end of relative openness, in Estonia they were also marked by the start of the "war of the wetlands," a campaign against massive drainage projects, the success of which led to the establishment of thirty mire reserves.[27] Even as social activism in the USSR was largely suppressed, collective action found an outlet in ostensibly apolitical movements promoting nature conservation. The scale of related mass-events is impressive and included large multi-day gatherings and bus-tours, but also smaller seminars and afternoon meetings, all undertaken in different locations (Figure 2 gives a sense of the high-spirited atmosphere of these gatherings).

The nature conservation movement was thoroughly intertwined with another mass activity: *kodu-uurimus*, the study of one's home region, an amateur-level investigation into regional history, language, and nature – in official publications,

**Figure 2** Meeting of the Nature Conservation Society of the ESSR at Kirbla Bank, with Jaan Eilart in the foreground. 1975. National Archives of Estonia, EFA.331.0.162131. Unknown photographer.

---

[27] "Soodesõda ei lõpe kunagi. Botaanik Ann Marvetit küsitlenud Toomas Kukk," *Eesti Loodus*, no. 9 (2010): 38. H. Kink, A. Raukas, and T. Kaasik, eds., *Eesti kaitsealad – Geoloogia ja vesi. Estonian Nature Protection Areas: Geology and Water* (Tallinn: Teaduste Akadeemia Kirjastus, 1996). The "war of the wetlands" also involved an "aesthetic education," that is, cultivating an appreciation for the beauty of swamps and marshes that a foreign observer might easily dismiss as landscapes lacking "charismatic fauna" – as in Alan Roe's brief remarks about Lahemaa, in Alan D. Roe, *Into Russian Nature: Tourism, Environmental Protection, and National Parks in the Twentieth Century* (New York: Oxford University Press, 2020), 84.

the two fields are often presented under one rubric.[28] Jaan Eilart, who shared his seemingly tireless energy between environmental action and *kodu-uurimus*, was deeply convinced of the necessity of a combined approach. "Nature is homely. And nature is cosmopolitan," declared Eilart.[29] Nature conservation in Estonia acknowledged its roots with the Baltic-Germans, tracing its origin to Gregor von Helmersen's 1879 calls to protect glacial erratic boulders, the majestic presence of which had given material to numerous folk legends and which have continued to fascinate and inspire artists, scholars, and ordinary visitors (see Figure 3).[30] Soviet-era *kodu-uurimus* in Estonia likewise located its origins with

**Figure 3** Vana-Jüri boulder on the Käsmu shore, around 1929. The Vana-Jüri boulder was placed under protection as a natural object in 1939 and again in the Soviet era in 1959. Unknown photographer. Estonian National Museum.

---

[28] The Estonian *kodu-uurimine* is related to the German *Heimatforschung*, the Finnish *kotiseututkimus*, and the Russian *krayevedeniye*. Interestingly, even as its German, Finnish, and Russian counterparts all refer to "regional research," the Estonian term gives no sense of "region" at all – it is literally just "home-study." As terms, the German "Heimat" and Finnish "koti" do both include resonances of "home," while the Russian term refers simply to regional studies without any resonance of home.

[29] Jaan Eilart, *Õitse ja haljenda. Eesti mõttelugu 129. Tartu: Ilmamaa, 2016*, ed. Andres Tõnisson and Taavi Pae (Tartu: Ilmamaa, 2016), 80.

[30] Karl Orviku, "Akadeemik G. Helmersen ja suurte rändrahnude kaitse," *Eesti Loodus*, no. 1 (1970): 43–44.

**Figure 4** A gathering of home-region researchers, 11–14 July 1974. At the foot of Jaani-Tooma boulder in Kasispea village, Lahemaa. Photographer Lembit Valgemäe. National Archives of Estonia, EAA.5266.1.1271.164

eighteenth-century Baltic-German intellectuals.[31] As a mass activity, however, it was institutionalized in the late nineteenth century and had established a solid standing for itself prior to the Soviet annexation.[32] Under Soviet rule, it was able to continue with official support – German *Heimatkunde* had also already inspired the development of Russian *krayevedeniye* in the nineteenth century – which then became, after the revolution, strongly promoted at the state level all over the USSR (see Figure 4 for one 1974 gathering of home-region researchers).[33]

Combined forms of nature-related activism – whether in environmental work or in studies of one's home region – involved an impressive number of participants. The October 1970 issue of the nature magazine *Eesti Loodus*, for example, provides information about four republic-level gatherings of environmentalists and home-region researchers in June and July 1970: the affiliated members of the Estonian Society for Nature Research met on June 6–8 with about a hundred participants; home-region researchers met on June 7–10 with about two hundred participants; the 9th Estonian Naturalists' Day met on 25–26 July

---

[31] *Erikursus kodu-uurimuse alused* (Tartu: Tartu Riiklik Ülikool, 1970).
[32] Hans Kruus, "Kodu-uurimise olukorrast ja ülesannetest Eesti NSV-S," *Eesti NSV Teaduste Akadeemia toimetised. Ühiskonnateaduste seeria* 8, no. 3 (1959): 279–95.
[33] Sofia Gavrilova, "Redefining the Soviet Krayevedeniye: The Role of Spatial Science in the Soviet System of Knowledge Production," *Journal of Historical Geography* 75 (2022): 14–23.

with more than 250 participants; and a gathering of the Estonian Nature Protection Society met on 25–26 July with more than 400 participants. All these events included presentations and excursions; the last event included a visit to the grave of the poet August Sang.[34]

Traditions and rituals helped bond participants together and strengthen the sense of cultural continuity: at the last hour of New Years Eve, the Tartu Students' Nature Conservation Circle went to light candles at the graves of nature conservation and cultural figures (Gregor Helmersen, Karl Ernst von Baer, and others), and then welcomed the New Year on historic Toomemägi.[35]

## Global Concern over Pollution: *Silent Spring* by Rachel Carson

The Estonian environmental movement was part of a global trend, of course; in 1970, the European Conservation Year campaign gave further impetus to environmental action in Estonia.[36] By the mid- to late twentieth century, pollution in many parts of the world had forced an environmental reckoning, the urgency of which spread both locally and globally. *Silent Spring* (1962), by the American marine biologist and writer Rachel Carson, was widely discussed in the United States, Canada, and all over Europe and is widely considered to have launched the modern environmental movement as a mass movement. Carson provided a comprehensive popular scientific overview of the detrimental impact of pesticides on the natural environment, and she also voiced concern over the impact of radioactive nuclear fallout. In 1962, she gave a stark, credible warning: "It is only within the moment of time represented by the twentieth century that one species – man – has acquired significant power to alter the nature of his world, and it is only within the past twenty-five years that this power has achieved such magnitude that it endangers the whole earth and its life."[37]

Carson's book generated a massive response, including fierce opposition from the chemical industry and others, but it also led to changes in US pesticide regulations. The urgent import of this and similar texts came to influence debates in the Soviet Union, including the Estonian SSR. Notwithstanding her death in 1964, Carson's was an influential voice in the context of Estonia in the 1960s and 1970s – Ain Kaalep's 1965 essay, to cite one example, borrows from Carson's established prestige to add legitimacy to Schweitzer's, observing that Carson's famous book drew its inspiration from Schweitzer's ideas – and,

---

[34] "Kroonika," *Eesti Loodus*, no. 10 (1970): 639.
[35] Jaan Eilart, "Viis aastat Tartu Üliõpilaste Looduskaitseringi," in *Looduskaitsealaseid töid. Pühendatud Tartu Üliõpilaste Looduskaitseringi 5. aastapäevale*, ed. Jaan Eilart (Tartu: Tartu Riiklik Ülikool, 1963), 107.
[36] This was the first trans-European annual effort of its kind.
[37] Rachel Carson, "Silent Spring – 1," *The New Yorker*, June 9, 1962.

indeed, *Silent Spring* is dedicated to Schweitzer and borrows its motto from his work, and allegedly Carson kept a photo of Schweitzer on her desk.[38]

It was through Carson's writing that, even before September 1965, Estonian readers had heard Schweitzer's name in environmentalist contexts: the journal *Eesti Loodus* printed a translation of a section of Carson's book in June 1965, together with a lengthy introduction. Carson referred to Schweitzer, whom she much admired; this section was later, in 1966, reprinted in the daily newspaper *Edasi*, which for more than a month issued serial selections from Carson's book. The book as a whole was finally published in full-length Estonian translation in 1968 (see Figure 5) – three years after the Russian translation of 1965.

**Figure 5** The cover of the Estonian translation of Carson's Silent Spring. Tallinn: Valgus, 1968. Design by Tõnis Laanemaa.

---

[38] Ara Paul Barsam, *Reverence for Life: Albert Schweitzer's Great Contribution to Ethical Thought* (Oxford: Oxford University Press, 2008), x.

**Figure 6** Ilmar Torn. Silent Spring. 1970. Woodcut. Tartu Art Museum.

Carson's poetic imagery – notably the silent spring itself, a spring devoid of birdsong – inspired a number of Estonian poets and artists. The oeuvre of artist Ilmar Torn includes a woodcut titled *Silent Spring* (1970) (Figure 6), and, beginning in the mid- and late 1960s, many other Estonian artists found resonance in the themes of environmental devastation.[39]

## Contesting Russian Perspectives

Carson's influence appeared most powerfully in motivating environmental action; Schweitzer, somewhat by contrast, became part of more general, philosophically attuned conversations about ethics, responsibility, and care for all living beings, among Estonian authors. Schweitzer's "reverence for life" served to bridge local and global ethical perspectives: it supported the articulation of an

---

[39] Linda Kaljundi, "Kunst, keskkond ja keskkonnaliikumine Eestis 1960.–1980. aastatel – Mõningatest hästi unustatud seostest ja suundumustest," *Methis. Studia Humaniora Estonica* 30 (2022): 92–116; Linda Kaljundi and Karin Vicente, eds., *Kunst Antropotseeni ajastul = Art in the Age of the Anthropocene* (Tallinn: Eesti Kunstimuuseum, 2023).

affective relationship to the surrounding environment, but it also linked Estonian concerns to global environmental ideas and values.[40]

Schweitzer's popularity and the reach of his influence in the USSR stretched well beyond the Baltics; indeed his Baltic success was conditioned upon his legitimation by the centers of Soviet power. Especially after his death in 1965, Schweitzer came to be widely talked about and translated in the USSR as a promoter of peace and nuclear disarmament and as an anti-colonial thinker.[41] An essay by the important Russian sociologist Yuri Levada *A. Shveitser—Myslitel' i chelovek* [*A. Schweitzer – the Thinker and the Person*], published in the journal *Voprosy Filosofii*, 1965, suggests a rather different figure than the one that inspired the Estonians, however. For Levada, Schweitzer was an old-fashioned thinker, mired in an outdated religiosity and incapable of offering anything new for thought. If Schweitzer embodied an extraordinary combination of high moral values and personal commitment, nonetheless, for Levada, Schweitzer was an unworldly figure, akin to Don Quixote. Levada passingly refers to Schweitzer's *Reverence for Life*, yet dismisses it as flourish of Schweitzer's more general religiosity.[42]

Estonian writers disagreed. In 1966, Eerik Kumari pointedly declared that Schweitzer was "not at all old-fashioned."[43] Ain Kaalep's short 1967 essay does not mention Levada by name, but it reads as a full refutation of his argument. Kaalep's essay was published in an unexpected venue: a nature-themed wall calendar: amid poems and lyric descriptions of natural phenomena, Schweitzer was the only figure thus singled out.[44] "That Albert Schweitzer had a theological education, should not disturb people with a clear mind," writes Kaalep.[45] Religion, he observed, has historically emphasized the principle of honoring life in different parts of the world. Moreover, "Albert Schweitzer was anything but a hermit of the primeval forest," Kaalep writes, emphasizing that Schweitzer's active involvement in the struggle against nuclear brinkmanship brought him into the midst of the most vital politics of the day.[46] Kaalep briefly sums up his case: "Reverence for life is among the most important slogans of our century."[47]

Estonian authors also declined to reproduce official Russian presentations of Schweitzer as a critique specific to capitalist societies. Take the 1973

---

[40] Similar ideas continue to circulate in the field of environmental research: Dipesh Chakrabarty's monograph has subsections "Modernity and the Loss of Reverence" and "Wonder and Reverence." Chakrabarty does not refer to Schweitzer, however. Dipesh Chakrabarty, *The Climate of History in a Planetary Age* (Chicago: University of Chicago Press, 2021), 194–204.
[41] Russian-language Schweitzeriana includes also several biographies.
[42] Iurii Levada, "A. Shveitser—Myslitel' i chelovek," *Voprosy Filosofii*, no. 12 (1965): 91–98.
[43] Kumari, "Kaitsta elu."
[44] Ain Kaalep, "Aukartus elu ees ja Albert Schweitzer," in Looduse kalender 1968 (Tallinn: Valgus, 1967).
[45] Kaalep.   [46] Kaalep.   [47] Kaalep.

introduction to the Russian translation of Schweitzer's *Kultur und Ethik* (*Civilization and Ethics*): Vladimir Karpushin locates Schweitzer's ideas within the official Marxist-Leninist paradigm and claims Schweitzer as a critic of the "great social tragedy" – namely the cultural crisis of modern bourgeois society. According to Karpushin, "The way out of this crisis was provided by the theory of Marxism, the end to this tragedy of culture is brought by socialism."[48] Karpushin's Marxist contextualization thus sought to affirm Schweitzer as a thinker in tune with the values of the Soviet state. Estonian writers, by contrast, desisted from the effort to externalize Schweitzer's critique as of special pertinence to bourgeois societies in other places; rather than proclaiming their satisfaction with the Soviet version of state socialism, they identified themselves as denizens of a global world that had reached "an ethical bankruptcy" and threatened "life on Earth with collapse."[49] Such thoroughly pessimistic visions of humankind were also expressed in visual arts: in the mixed media work *Pollution* by Olev Soans, for example, a suffering human figure is surrounded by both high-tech space vehicles and by a bare Earth littered with trash cans (Figure 7).

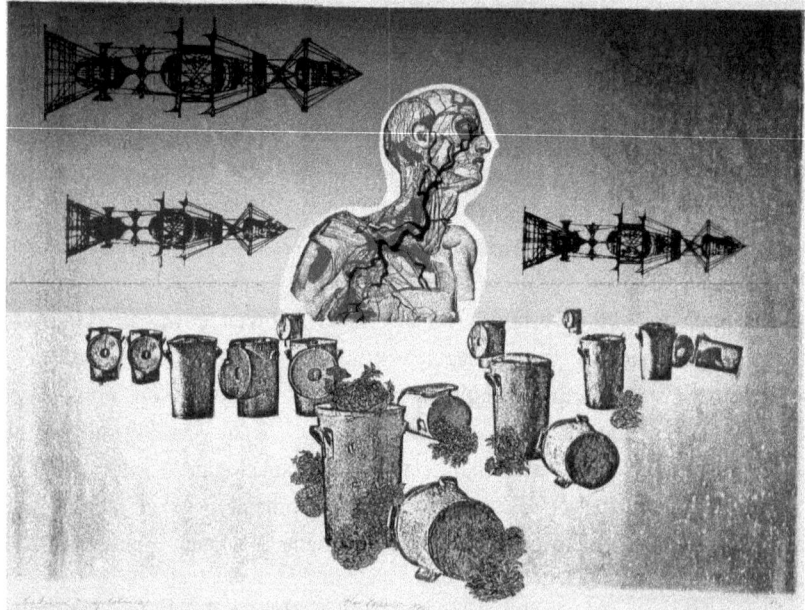

**Figure 7** Olev Soans. Pollution. 1973. Mixed media on paper. Art Museum of Estonia.

---

[48] Vladimir Karpushin, "Predisloviye," in Albert Shveitser, *Kul'tura i etika*, ed. (Moskva: Progress, 1973), 29.

[49] Jaan Kaplinski, "Eelarvamused ja eetika. Utoopilisi mõtisklusi," *Looming*, no. 12 (1968): 1865.

## The Critique of Soviet Agriculture

In 1969, Jaan Eilart directed his criticism against the industrial cultivation of virgin lands: when humans start challenging the inflexible laws of nature, he argued, then the ancient laws of nature will assert their prerogatives – and so it may come to pass that "the endless virgin lands ploughed into fallows will remain soilless," that water will become too tainted to quench anyone's thirst, and that the eagle will be unable find a forest for its nesting.[50] Such themes were further explored in critical documentaries about Soviet-style agriculture, the first of these being *Võõras higi* [*Someone Else's Sweat, 1973*], directed by Jüri Müür. A more prominent example was the film *Ärge tapke vihmaussi* [*Do Not Kill the Earthworm*, 1978], directed by Heli Speek, which shows how the crushing weight of massive agricultural machinery alters the structure of the soil and severely endangers the soil-aerating earthworms. *Künnimehe väsimus* [*The Plowman's Fatigue*], another documentary directed by Jüri Müür, was even more pointed in its criticism – with the result that the 1982 film, though winning festival awards, got stuck in the censorship machine and reached general audiences only in 1986, two years after the death of its director.

After *Künnimehe väsimus* received first prize at the Agricultural Film Festival in Alma-Ata (now Almaty, Kazakhstan), Jüri Müür told a journalist, "The chairman of the Kazakh Film Committee, for example, stated that, in the past ten years, he has seen no film so thrilling as this one, be it a feature film or otherwise."[51] While Speek's and Müür's visions of the suffering soil and frustrated kolkhoz workers went starkly against the grain of official Russian virgin-land optimism, one could find parallel themes in Estonian art (see Figure 8), and in works by film directors from other Soviet republics. The film *Znoi* [*Heat*, 1963], directed by Ukrainian filmmaker Larissa Shepitko and produced by Kirgizfilm on motifs from a Chingiz Aitmatov's short story, included such bitter visual critique that Mieka Erley has called this film "an indexical document of the erosion of the fragile topsoil of Kazakhstan's virgin land."[52] Only professional audiences in Kazakhstan were able to see Müür's film, yet the fate of Shepitko's film in Estonia was scarcely any better: Soviet films typically played to near-empty theatres at Estonian cinemas. Thus, the critic Ardi Liives, who admitted that it was quite accidentally that he saw the film himself, lamented that Shepitko's masterful film came and went, virtually unnoticed by Estonian audiences.[53]

---

[50] Jaan Eilart, "Loodus kultuuris," *Sirp ja Vasar*, January 31, 1969.
[51] Enn Kalda, "Üleliiduline esikoht Eesti dokfilmile," *Sirp ja Vasar*, May 6, 1983.
[52] Mieka Erley, *On Russian Soil: Myth and Materiality* (Ithaca: Northern Illinois Press/Cornell University Press, 2021), chap. 124.
[53] Ardi Liives, "Mõni sõna filmist, selle vaatajast ja kriitikast," *Sirp ja Vasar*, November 15, 1963.

**Figure 8** The devastated fields found their way into the exhibition halls: Jüri Palm, Soil in Drought. 1971. Oil on canvas. Art Museum of Estonia.

## Not Only the Environment: Reverence for Life in Times of the Destruction of Democracy

One of the most striking references to Schweitzer in the Soviet Estonian media comes in the context of the 1968 invasion of Czechoslovakia. On August 21, 1968, Soviet troops and their allies entered Czechoslovakia to violently suppress its processes of democratization. Two weeks later, in the September 6th issue of the newspaper *Edasi*, a photo of the young and extremely popular writer Mati Unt dominates the front page. Unt writes at length about peace-loving hippies, comparing them to the earlier Beat Generation, but he emphasizes their commitment to peace:

> Hippies, the "long-haired ones," fight against violence (the familiar slogans promoting non-violence), no matter the form of its appearance: militarism, police, gangsterism, hooliganism, environmental destruction, animal cruelty.

[...] The hippies' role models are India's national hero Mahatma Gandhi, with his ideology of passive resistance, as well as Christ, Buddha, Diogenes, Henry David Thoreau (immersing oneself in nature), and Albert Schweitzer ("reverence for life").[54]

Unt's repeated special emphasis in this text is on the ethical position of hippies: it is not, as it might seem, long hair that defines a hippie, it's an ethics of living.

*Edasi* ran Unt's article in parallel with a column of TASS news pieces from Czechoslovakia. Deaths and arrests are not mentioned in these official bulletins – one declares, for example, in response to queries from international PEN-club and other organizations, that various Czechoslovakian cultural figures are "working normally and taking an active part in the social life of their country."[55] The layout poses Unt's piece as a clear judgment against the military aggression in Czechoslovakia. Schweitzer had joined with Gandhi, Thoreau, and the hippies to highlight to the readers of Edasi the imperial violence of the Soviet regime.

## An Estonian Schweitzer – Jaan Kaplinski on Wonder, Care, and Responsibility

Among Estonian writers, the eminent poet Jaan Kaplinski stands forth as most deeply marked by Schweitzer's ideas: Kaplinski makes detailed reference to Schweitzer's work in a number of his essays, and, for his massive 2004 volume of collected essays, he chose a title that paraphrased Schweitzer's famous dictum.[56] Kaplinski himself was among the leading critical thinkers in Tartu intellectual circles, a polyglot who read and translated from many languages and was later nominated for the Nobel Prize in literature (Figure 9). He was deeply interested in indigenous cultures in different parts of the world, yet he was also very much invested in modern poetry, and throughout his oeuvre he addressed environmental concerns. Jaan Eilart noted in 1976 that Kaplinski creates "in Estonian conditions, a comprehensive and deeply felt system, which, in our circumstances, is as meaningful as Mahatma Gandhi's and Albert Schweitzer's philosophies of reverence for life."[57]

When Jaan Kaplinski writes about natural environments, he does so with an emphasis on the sense of wonder, on seeing the world more fully, and on the necessity for moving with cautious respect toward everything living.[58] In his

---

[54] Mati Unt, "Pikad juuksed, lühike aru?," Edasi, September 6, 1968.
[55] "Tšehhoslovakkia SV Siseministeeriumi avaldus," *Edasi*, September 6, 1968.
[56] Jaan Kaplinski, *Kõik on ime*, ed. Thomas Salumets (Tartu: Ilmamaa. e-raamat, 2004).
[57] Jaan Eilart, *Inimene, ökosüsteem ja kultuur. Peatükke looduskaitsest Eestis* (Tallinn: Perioodika, 1976).
[58] Such affinities are obviously not restricted to Baltic literatures. Within the wider Soviet sphere, comparisons can be made with Leonid Leonov's novel *Russkiy les (Russian Forest)*, the works of canonical Kirgiz author Chingiz Aitmatov, and many others. See also Alec Brookes and Elena

**Figure 9** Jaan Kaplinski. Poetry night at the café of Tartu State University. 1970. Photographer Harry Karro. Estonian Literature Museum.

1968 essay *Eelarvamused ja eetika. Utoopilisi mõtisklusi* [*Prejudices and Ethics: Utopian Contemplations*], Kaplinski counterposes the Cartesian disregard for the nonhuman with Schweitzer's "Reverence for Life," which Kaplinski glosses as "a wonderment toward the life unfolding in all beings and a commitment to defend this life."[59] He envisions a future world in which a peaceful balance has been established in nature and in human-animal interactions: "Wild birds will fly in the homes of these future human beings and deer and giraffe will peer inside their windows."[60] The 1968 essay affirms a cautiously optimistic tone: Kaplinski seems to be sincerely hopeful about the "progress of the human conscience" over the course of time and about the possibility of grounding human existences within their natural environments upon an ethical reverence for life.[61] By 1973, Kaplinski's tone has changed: his *Mõtisklusi inimkultuurist ja ökosüsteemidest [Thoughs about Human Culture and Ecological Systems]* issues a warning about the human capacity for destruction in an era of advanced technologies.[62]

In his 1972 essay *Ökoloogia ja ökonoomika* [*Ecology and Economy*] Kaplinski again foregrounds the position of care and reverence:

---

Fratto, eds., "The Anthropocene and Russian Literature. Special Issue," *Russian Literature* 114–115 (2020).

[59] Kaplinski, "Eelarvamused ja eetika. Utoopilisi mõtisklusi," 1861.  [60] Kaplinski, 1865.
[61] Kaplinski, 1862–63.
[62] Jaan Kaplinski, "Mõtisklusi inimkultuurist ja ökosüsteemidest," *Eesti Loodus*, no. 9 (1973): 569.

Without even noticing, we will start stepping more quietly, so as not to disturb the hazel grouse with her chicks or the pike spying at us from under the leaf of a water lily. We will become more modest, more cautious, and smaller. And yet we will begin to see more, to partake in more than when we rushed through the forest and through the world in a clamorous hurry.[63]

The attitude of wonder and care toward natural environments and all living beings is again associated with Schweitzer's "Reverence for Life" – an attitude that, according to Kaplinski, many follow, if only implicitly – after all, "a person does not express or talk about things taken for granted."[64] Yet those who avoid disturbing the ants in their path or who leave a viper unharmed are proceeding from the same impulse of care, awe, and reverence.[65]

An important theme in Kaplinski's environmental writings is the scope of one's self-world. As Kaplinski describes it, developed modern societies, both capitalist and socialist, have constricted human consciousness. Indeed, in this respect Kaplinski does not distinguish between capitalist and socialist societies – both manifest a cultural logic dominated by the drive for economic growth.

Kaplinski juxtaposes an ethical care for all living beings and all natural environments – reverence for life – with societal efforts to accelerate economic growth in the industrial era, with the production of new needs and new products to satisfy these needs, and, as a result, with new cultural value-systems that place their emphasis on the accumulation of goods.[66] Profound identification with one's environment and so also the model of a 'spacious selfhood' were, in Kaplinski's account, characteristic of the pre-industrial era – in pre-industrial times, the constitutive relationship between self and environment extended far beyond the world directly sensed and experienced. Industrial societies, by contrast, have precipitated "a shrinkage of the self";[67] the task is now to re-extend the self and recover some extent of its former scope. In the essay *Ökoloogia ja ökonoomika* [*Ecology and Economy*] Kaplinski writes:

> We want what is beautiful and precious to be our "own," close to us, within the reach of hand and eye. [...] We dress well, we furnish our apartments as

---

[63] Jaan Kaplinski, "Ökoloogia ja ökonoomika", *See ja teine* (Tallinn, 2013) 79–80. Kaplinski's essay remained unpublished until 1996; it is not known how widely the manuscript may have circulated before its publication.

[64] Kaplinski, 54.

[65] Kaplinski, 53–54. For Kaplinski himself, a far greater impact than Schweitzer's was left by the Estonian religious philosopher Uku Masing, his mentor who lived in internal exile, unable to make public use of his erudition. There was an important affinity between Masing's and Schweitzer's views: Both felt close to the nonliving world, both found inspiration in Eastern religions, and both were highly critical of Western colonialism. Salumets, *Unforced Flourishing: Understanding Jaan Kaplinski*, 89–100; Sven Vabar, *Uurimus Uku Masingu tõest. Magistritöö* (Tartu: Eesti Digiraamatute Keskus, 2007).

[66] Kaplinski, "Ökoloogia ja ökonoomika," 62.   [67] Kaplinski, "Ökoloogia ja ökonoomika," 72.

nicely as we can. If the house belongs to us, we embellish it too, yet we relegate the street and the city to oblivion, almost without giving any thought at all to the plurification and beautification of the landscape – it appears that the limits of our selves can be measured within a couple of meters, sometimes perhaps a couple dozen meters, but rarely more.

It seems that human being itself has, in recent centuries, suffered a significant contraction of its boundaries.[68]

In Kaplinski's analysis, the diminution of the modern self proceeds from its indifference to environmental problems and an impoverished sense of responsibility: "Perhaps we have shrunk the self to its bare minimum, in order to shirk responsibility for our ecological misdeeds, to disavow them as at an 'exterior' remove."[69]

Kaplinski's writings present an environmentally conscious subject who identifies through a direct, affectively experienced environment, but who also realizes the intrication of local, global, and planetary processes. Such a subject feels, most immediately, a belonging-together with their directly sensible surroundings, including natural environments, but they also acknowledge the unity of all living and nonliving matter. The binding link between different scales of subjecthood is provided by care and concern: in this sense, the subject is constituted by relations of care, as these extend from the intimate to the planetary and beyond.

Kaplinski's writings skip across their different scales, sometimes lingering on closely knit self-worlds, and sometimes extending to embrace a planetary wholeness. The global often appears as the more distressed side of the story – the site of global pollution and the devastation caused by shortsighted industrial policies and the desire for short-term profit, something common to both capitalist and socialist world-orders.

In this mental framework, references to the particularities of the Soviet regime are marginal, if present at all. It would be an insult to call Kaplinski "a Soviet writer," even as he happened to live and write under Soviet rule. In the environmentally attuned life of Kaplinski and many others, Sovietness was but one obligatory aspect of life – and not the defining one.

## From an Ethics of Care to Cosmic Visions, Surpassing Eco-nationalism

At times, Kaplinski's writing also strives for a cosmic scale, a critical vision of the Earth and global problems as seen from the perspective of outer space. In the 1960s, the first golden age of space exploration, visions of the Earth from space

---

[68] Kaplinski, 70.  [69] Kaplinski, 73.

and the possibility of encountering extraterrestrial civilizations were widely popular topics all over the Soviet Union and elsewhere in the globalized world. Soviet science fiction was booming, of course, and other examples abound: in Vasily Aksyonov's novel *Zvyozdny bilet* [*Ticket to the Stars,* 1961], Dimka dreams about a "cosmic friendship among nations"; in Mati Unt's *Elu võimalikkusest kosmoses* [*About the Possibility of Life in Space,* 1967], the character Ester imagines that there might be someone out there in space seeking to make contact through a late-night television channel.[70] By the late 1970s, these themes found pessimistic expression and acquired existential depth, but their popularity continued apace. Chingiz Aitmatov's novel *I dol'she veka dlitsya den'* [*The Day Lasts Longer Than a Hundred Years,* 1980] was read and staged in theatres (including in two Estonian theatres) all over the Soviet Union: Aitmatov provides an ecologically sensitive epic vision, in which life on a harmonious green-thinking planet Lesnaya Grud' is juxtaposed with Earth's power struggles and its rampant carelessness toward nature and heritage. Deeply devastated by the shrinkage of the Aral Sea and by restrictions imposed by Russian-speaking colonial order, Aitmatov's local Kazakh characters nevertheless retain strong connection to their local environment and traditions.[71]

In 1968, Kaplinski expresses concern that human explorations of outer space might regress into just another version of exploitative colonialism. The poet imagines alien cultures assessing the "cosmic ethical maturity" on Earth "according to our ability to sustain and protect everything that lives."[72] The cosmic perspective displays human failures of care as an egregious ethical lapse: "Once we can accustom ourselves to thinking in a cosmic perspective, even if gradually, the misjudgments and inconsistencies in earthly matters appear in an even more disturbing and irrational light."[73]

Jaan Kaplinski, Ain Kaalep, Jaan Eilart and many others articulated and reflected, each in their own way, common feelings and worries that were abundantly present in fiction, life-writing, visual arts, media discourse, and popular imagination. As the ecological situation had become dire in many respects, environmental concerns came to be voiced more frequently and more openly. In 1970, in response to an interviewer's question concerning the state of water protection in the republic, the head of the Environmental agency in the Estonian SSR gave his blunt assessment, "The situation is very bad," and he listed "dead" bodies of water: Võrtsjärv lake and the Keila,

---

[70] Vasily Aksyonov, "Zvyozdny bilet," *Yunost'*, no. 6–7 (1961); Mati Unt, *Elu võimalikkusest kosmoses* (Tallinn: Perioodika, 1967).
[71] Chingiz Aitmatov, *I dol'she veka dlitsya den'* (Frunze: Kyrgyzstan, 1981).
[72] Kaplinski, "Eelarvamused ja eetika. Utoopilisi mõtisklusi," 1865.   [73] Kaplinski, 1865.

**Figure 10** Evi Tihemets, Endangered World. 1970. Etching and lithography on paper. Tartu Art Museum.

Võhandu, Põltsamaa, Pirita, Väike-Emajõgi, and Jänijõgi rivers.[74] It was also no secret that the Baltic Sea was "among the most ravaged ecosystems."[75] Visual artists also reflected such concerns: see, for example, the austere, desiccated plant world in Evi Tihemets's lithography *Endangered World* (Figure 10).

A shared ethical vision of the interconnectedness of all living beings, bound to intimate sensations of awe and reverence, but colored by deep concern for unabated processes of environmental devastation – such was the personal-global-planetary undercurrent of the era.

Since the publication of Jane Dawson's book *Eco-Nationalism* in 1996, environmental movements in Eastern European societies have been treated with a certain skepticism, with environmentalism in the region presumed to amount to little more than surrogate nationalism, something to be discarded as soon as more overtly nationalist sentiments are able to be expressed without

---
[74] "Looduskaitsepäeva Intervjuu," *Eesti Loodus*, no. 5 (1970): 259.
[75] Jaan Eilart, *Inimene, ökosüsteem ja kultuur. Peatükke looduskaitsest Eestis* (Tallinn: Perioodika, 1976), 53.

coercive repression. Dawson characterizes perestroika-era anti-nuclear activism in Lithuania, Armenia, and Tatarstan as movement-surrogacy, or, "the hiding of political intentions behind an apparently nonthreatening cause."[76] Such surrogate activism, Dawson argues, is discarded as soon as new opportunities allow the "activists' true agenda" to be openly displayed.[77] As Dawson explains, "the eco-nationalist phenomenon implies a certain superficiality," as nationalists mask "their intentions behind a surrogate cause."[78]

While this Element will make no claims about "the Soviet case," as Dawson sweepingly refers to her own material, I hope that this section has demonstrated that the scope of environmental thought and activism in Soviet-era Estonia gives no ground for accusations of surrogate eco-nationalism.[79] Environmentalism in the Soviet Union was not merely a surrogate phenomenon of the perestroika-era decolonial nationalism, but should be understood in its local specificities, transnational connectedness, engagement with global concerns, and through its long-term developments.

*My parents had both Rachel Carson's* Silent Spring *and two volumes of essays by Albert Schweitzer on our bookshelves. These books are now with me, in another home, in an old farmhouse on Saaremaa island, Estonia. As I put finishing touches to this section in June 2023, a fox looks at me, pausing briefly in its leisurely walk across the hay field at dusk. A moment ago, two young deer were frisking about. Earlier today, the tractor gathered the dried hay, bound it together, and then spat it into great balls. These balls smell the same as the haylofts of my childhood.*

*The farm homes in our village, some for year-round habitation, others turned into summer homes, have seen several changes of regimes and times. The walls and the living room floor of this house date back to the early twentieth century. A new thatch roof was built ten years ago, using traditional techniques. There is spring by the edge of the hay field, hidden under the trees – its little jets of fresh water have burst forth for time out of mind, as have the winds blowing from the sea, less than two kilometers distant. The evening is quiet; the world is light and still.*

---

[76] Jane Dawson, *Eco-Nationalism: Anti-Nuclear Activism and National Identity in Russia, Lithuania, and Ukraine* (Durham: Duke University Press, 1996), 18. Even as eco-nationalism has become something of a generic pejorative buzzword for Eastern European environmentalism, Dawson herself acknowledges some variation: in Ukraine, the anti-nuclear movement was "a catalyst for nationalism rather than a surrogate," and "in Ukraine, environmental and nationalist goals were mutually reinforcing" (p. 79). Dawson associates this with a weaker sense of national identity in Ukraine; according to her dismissive (and mistaken) assessment, in Ukraine, in 1991, "independence was suddenly tossed into their laps" (p. 78).

[77] Ibid., 19.   [78] Ibid., 163.

[79] For a critique of Dawson's movement surrogacy, see, for example, Katrina Z. S. Schwartz, *Nature and National Identity after Communism: Globalizing the Ethnoscape* (Pittsburgh: University of Pittsburgh Press, 2006).

*Elsewhere, icebergs are slowly melting, and the Ukrainian people defend their land against Russian invasion. If anyone out in space were to assess our "cosmic ethical maturity [...] according to our ability to sustain and protect everything that lives,"*[80] *it is hard to imagine that we would pass that test.*

## 2 The Forbidden Sea and Colonial Violence. 1976

### Letipea, August 8, 1976

On August 7, 1976, gas company workers from all over the Estonian SSR came together for their annual summer gathering, held that year in Letipea, on the north coast of Estonia, at a training and vacation complex for auxiliary traffic inspectors, but regularly used for events such as this. Throughout the Soviet decades, the western islands and the whole northern coastline of Estonia, including Letipea, were part of the Soviet border zone, heavily militarized and patrolled and with stringent restrictions regulating access. But because no successful escapes to the "free world" across the sea had taken place since the 1950s, and because the sea itself was monitored with extreme vigilance, border zone regulations had become somewhat more relaxed by the mid-1970s.[81] One important development in this process had been the establishment of Lahemaa National Park in 1971, which we mentioned in Section 1: the status of the national park granted limited access to many areas on the northern shoreline that until then had been closed to the general population. Arne Kaasik, who began work as an environmental inspector in the national park in 1972, recollected that it was at this time that people were finally allowed to go to the Lahemaa seashore, and even to celebrate midsummer night there.[82]

Letipea, however, was not part of Lahemaa National Park. The gas workers and their families were thus given a very strict directive not to leave the camp area. Nearby was a well-known geological landmark, Ehalkivi (Figure 11), the largest glacial erratic boulder in Estonia and one of the largest in Northern Europe, with a volume of 930 m$^3$ – according to one folk tale, it was thrown there by the legendary hero Kalevipoeg; according to another, by the devil himself, all the way from Finland. The gas workers could not go near the giant bolder.

---

[80] Kaplinski, "Eelarvamused ja eetika. Utoopilisi mõtisklusi," 1865.
[81] Indrek Paavle, "Kuidas ära hoida „nõukogudevastaste elementide karistamatu lahkumine," ENSV territooriumilt? Piirirežiimi regulatsioon ja kontroll Eesti NSV-S," *Tuna*, no. 2 (2012); 61–91; Jaak Pihlau, "Lehekülgi Eesti lähiajaloost. Merepõgenemised okupeeritud Eestist," *Tuna*, no. 2 (2001): 68–81; Külvi Kuusk and Maivi Kärginen, *Stopp! Piiritsoon / Stop! Border Zone* (Tallinn: Rannarahva Muuseum, 2013).
[82] Rein Sikk, "Lahemaa Rahvuspark loodi Leninit tsiteerides," *Eesti Päevaleht*, December 10, 2007. www.delfi.ee/artikkel/17666394/lahemaa-rahvuspark-loodi-leninit-tsiteerides.

*Environment and Society in Soviet Estonia*

**Figure 11** Ehalkivi in 2016. Photo by Marko Vainu. Creativecommons.org.

The participants of the 1976 Letipea gathering, 344 people, including family members, camped in tents. An officer from the nearby garrison of border troops came over at the start of the festivities and checked in to find that everything was in good order. After some friendly sporting competitions and a concert, the evening was spent with dance, singing, and socializing. Food and alcohol were available for purchase on site. In addition to participants affiliated with the gas company, locals from the surrounding areas joined their acquaintances in what felt like a great party. One local inhabitant, Taima Kivilo, who had joined her friends at their tent, recalled a beautiful night: "Someone had an accordion and we sang and sang and sang …"[83] Kivilo's child, together with other local children, mingled with campers from elsewhere in Estonia – in the late hours, the children gathered inside one of the resort buildings.

Later in the evening, two border guards came and imposed themselves upon the gas workers' festivities. According to the story that would circulate later, one of them had received a sizeable sum of money from home, facilitating a three-day drinking binge, and the now thoroughly inebriated border guards

---

[83] Mati Talvik and Indrek Kangur, "Letipea veresaun." – Ajavaod 8. 7.11.2010, 2010. https://arhiiv.err.ee/vaata/ajavaod-letipea-veresaun [checked 13.09.2023]. Talvik and Kangur provide a thorough overview of the event, with multiple witness accounts and references to archival documents.

demanded "vodka and women" from the campers.[84] Conflict ensued. According to the unpublished official report, "Some of the participants in the gathering spoke with the border guards and asked them to leave peaceably, observing that it was inappropriate for the troops to be drunk while on duty."[85] The situation escalated from there.

The fatal hour arrived around 1:30 am on August 8, when most people were already in their tents for the night's rest. One of the drunken border guards opened fire, emptying four clips of ammunition, with altogether 100 shots, toward the tents and campers. "Because shots were fired low and only about four meters away from the tents, there were casualties even among those who were sleeping," reads the report.[86] Karin Paas, whose husband died in Letipea, later recalled the shouts of men urging people to *get down! get down!* and to hide in the forest.[87] After the shooting ceased, sometime later, a voice from the loudspeakers asked those who had arrived in cars to fetch their first-aid kits. Ambulances arrived, morning came – yet people were not allowed to depart before "security bosses from Moscow" had arrived and given their permission to leave.

Funerals were held a few days later in different parts of Estonia. In Rakvere, the nearest large town with most participants, people would later recall that different funeral processions were kept separate in order to forestall mass protest.[88] One 16-year-old student from Rakvere First High School had come to Letipea at his brother's invitation. According to one circulating version, bullets struck him in the middle of a dance and he died on the spot; according to another, the youngster was just about to enter a tent where others were at rest, when bullets struck him down, there at the tent entrance.

In Kingissepp (now Kuressaare), on the island of Saaremaa, classmates of the deceased Ferdinand Tulit boldly ignored official efforts to keep the funeral out of public sight. According to the recollection of the victim's brother, "the whole town was there" at the funeral procession. Even as the boys threw ink pots at the building of the security services, the militia did not dare to intervene. The fury

---

[84] Maris Kangru, "Ühe mõrva jälgedes," *Virumaa Teataja*, January 25, 1994; Helmut Elstrok, "Kolmekümne aasta tagune Letipea veresaun jääb alatiseks meelde," *Virumaa Teataja*, August 8, 2006.

[85] The official report sent from the local party committee to the First Secretary of the Central Committee of the Estonian Communist Party is available in "Õiend traagilisest õnnetusjuhtumist Rakvere rajoonis Letipeal, 09.08.1976." ERAF, 2620.73.16, n.d., 8.

[86] "Õiend traagilisest õnnetusjuhtumist Rakvere rajoonis Letipeal, 09.08.1976." ERAF, 2620.73.16, 8.

[87] "20 aastat metsikust massimõrvast Letipea rannas," *Eesti Päevaleht*, August 9, 1996; Talvik and Kangur, "Letipea veresaun." – Ajavaod 8. 7.11.2010.

[88] The witness account of Tiina Tammer whose 16-year-old classmate died in Letipea. Talvik and Kangur, "Letipea veresaun." – Ajavaod 8. 7.11.2010.

of islanders was all the deeper in that people still remembered an earlier tragedy of 1972, when a border guard tried to rape a local girl, faced resistance from the mother, and then shot them both – in some versions of the story, two other sisters were shot as well. Another earlier shooting had happened on nearby Vilsandi island, with two local victims. Decades later people would still point out that Ferdinand Tulit, a young father, had not wanted to go to Letipea at all, but had been obliged to go as a member of the local orchestra.[89]

In Rakvere, relatives were very concerned about the young widow of the deceased Anatoli Paas; for two days afterward, she did not utter a word or give a cry.[90] There were victims from Paide, Pärnu, Narva, Tartu, Kunda, and Tapa – even as the official press was silent about the event, the news spread quickly across Estonia. The Voice of America covered it. Parents of children staying at the nearby Karepa pioneer camp drove in to check on their children – and older children at the camp heard full details of the event from local teens.[91] As there was no official coverage, the story spread in different versions with a varying or unknown number of victims. It was rumored that the commandant of the garrison shot himself just before the chairman of the KGB, Yuri Andropov, reached there from Moscow. In another widely circulating version, of the two border guards involved, the other was a Latvian who had tried to stop his comrade, only to be shot himself. As Enno Tammer later recollected, in the late 1980s, when he would mention spending summers in Letipea, people's first reaction always referred to the 1976 massacre.

After the collapse of Soviet rule, archival documents became available to historians. The drunk border guards, Viktor Bagizhev and Nikolai Povyshev, were both from Russia. According to witness testimony, Povyshev had tried to stop his drunk companion and was shot; with the last bullet, the shooter, Bagizhev, mortally wounded himself. The report admits, though, that its authors could not exclude the possibility that one of the campers may have grabbed the gun and shot one or both of the guards. There were twenty-four casualties among the campers, six of whom died.[92]

---

[89] Urmas Kiil, "Mälestusi Nõukogude armeega toimunud vahejuhtumitest," *Saarte Hääl*, March 29, 2009; Katrin Pauts, "Lõputu õudus: 33 aasta taguses veresaunas hukkunud noormehe haud pühiti maa pealt," *Õhtuleht*, August 18, 2009; Anna Komissarova, "'S puley v legkom neprosto zhit'. Pochemu sovetskiy pogranichnik vzyalsya za avtomat i rasstrelal estonskikh turistov," *Lenta.Ru*, April 9, 2022.

[90] Talvik and Kangur, "Letipea veresaun." – Ajavaod 8. 7.11.2010.

[91] Raivo Raina, "Karepa pioneerilaagri lapsed said jõhkrast veretööst teada juba järgmisel hommikul," *Virumaa Teataja*, August 8, 2006. Karepa Pioneer Camp, under tall pine trees and verging on the shore, was among the best known summer camps in Estonia; I myself went there as a child in the late 1970s.

[92] "Õiend traagilisest õnnetusjuhtumist Rakvere rajoonis Letipeal, 09.08.1976," ERAF, f. 2620, n. 73, s. 16, l. 7–10.

## Political and Cultural Contexts

The Letipea massacre was a one-of-a-kind event. In the post-Stalin era, no other encounter between Estonian locals and Soviet border troops ended in mass killing, even as conflicts involving alcohol and women did occasionally take place.[93] Nonetheless, this event, although exceptional in its number of fatalities, was emblematic of a more general, structural issue: the mass-scale restriction of people's access to the shore, and a nonlocal, Russian-speaking, armed border guard as the figure of violence and refusal.[94] This was the structure of colonial eco-social violence: the imposition of restrictions upon simple, everyday interactions with homely environments, restrictions that felt deeply unfair and utterly unnecessary.[95] Why was it forbidden for a mother to spend an afternoon at the seashore with her children? Why was it a crime to go swimming after 10 pm in evening, in the long midsummer Nordic nights when it hardly gets dark at all? Why couldn't young people make a bonfire and spend the night camping by the sea? As all these demands and threats were issued in Russian, by armed men who did not speak the local language, these restrictions were experienced as yet another repressive marker of "Russian rule," as the Soviet order was commonly referred to in everyday parlance. These refusals and restrictions birthed a rich oral narrative tradition, variously bitter, frightful, or comic, involving rude or violent encounters, disappointments, ruined pleasures, and close escapes – one can easily collect many hundreds of such stories from interviews, archival work, and published life stories. Soviet border troops were subordinate to the KGB and not part of the regular army – yet ordinary people saw no difference between the two and referred to both indiscriminately as "sõdurid": soldiers. Notably, the Estonian word "sõdurid" comes from "sõda," signifying war – the Estonian imagination thus easily linked these armed men with the full spectrum of war-related violence. Such a connection also meant that, in oral exchange, guarded military bases and Soviet border troops merged into one mass of restrictive nonlocal armed presence. Take the recollections by the literary critic Toomas Haug: the images from his childhood years easily slide from encounters with the border troops – whom he calls "Russian soldiers" – to

---

[93] One recurrent pattern seems to have involved armed border troops coming to local parties and then, in situations of conflict, threatening to resolve the conflict with a gun. Ann-Leena Miller, "Keep out! No Entry! Exploring the Soviet Military Landscape of the Coast of Estonia," in *SHS Web of Conferences*, vol. 63 (EDP Sciences, 2019), 6; Taavi Koppel, *Hiiumaa piiritsoon 1940–41 Ja 1944–91. Bakalaureusetöö* (Tartu: Tartu Ülikool, 2015), 32–33.

[94] In 1956, national units were dismantled in the Soviet armed forces; as a rule, therefore, Estonians were sent to perform their military service elsewhere, outside the Estonian SSR. Kristjan Luts, *Eestlastest ajateenijad ja ohvitserid Nõukogude Liidu relvajõududes 1956–1991* (Tartu: Tartu Ülikooli Kirjastus, 2017), 43–46.

[95] "Eco-social" conveys "the fundamental interdependence of societal and ecological contexts." Nancy Krieger, *Ecosocial Theory, Embodied Truths, and the People's Health* (New York: Oxford University Press, 2021), 17.

tales told, during a lightning storm one night, of the great burning of Tallinn, bombed by the Red Army in the war, and then to the child's frightened sense during the violent storm that "war was so very close."[96]

Those living near to military facilities not only contended with restrictions upon their movement, but also lived with the consequences of environmental destruction. The careless management of the Tapa military airfield led to profound environmental disaster. The groundwater became thoroughly polluted: petroleum and oil leaked from their tanks, and locals report that they were also simply poured into the ground. The water drawn from local wells could be set afire (Figure 12). Elsewhere, Suur-and Väike-Pakri islands became

**Figure 12** A woman in Tapa pumps the water well but gets only sludge. 1992. National Archives of Estonia, EFA.204.0.263421. Photographer Albert Truuväärt.

---

[96] Toomas Haug, *Mööda Koidu tänavat* (Tallinn: Eesti Keele Sihtasutus, 2014), 65.

shooting targets used by all Warsaw Pact countries: bombings damaged the ground, fires devastated the vegetation, and, as was common practice in the seaside military and border garrisons, untreated wastewater from the barracks was pumped directly into the sea.[97]

## Cultural Imaginaries of the Sea

While the full extent of the pollution was obscured until the departure of Soviet troops in 1994, the restrictions imposed upon seashore access clashed with values at the heart of Estonians' cultural self-perception. The Estonian coastline includes 1242 km of mainland coastline and an additional 2552 km of insular coastline, and the sea and its open shores have played a central role in Estonian culture, along with the forests and fields in the southern part of the country. The official flag of the Estonian SSR even used blue waves to symbolize the republic (the very similar flag of the Latvian SSR put wave symbolism to very similar use). Poems and paintings of the sea made rich contributions to the core imaginaries of Estonianness, as did the much-reproduced view of Tallinn's medieval towers as seen from a seaward approach – a view that rather few Estonians were able to enjoy in person over the Soviet years. We will see in the next section how choral songs often typified the Estonian sense of nationhood as bound to specific local environments: song itself was figured as being born on the shores of the homeland, from the music and the rumble of wind and waves, to then become a powerful force that would bind the nation together. In the 1967 words of Lennart Meri, later the president of Estonia after it regained its independence, "we all carry within us the traces of the sea."[98]

Meri opens his highly influential, poetically imagined, book-length essay *Hõbevalge* [*Silver White*, 1967] by imagining Estonians' ancestral tribes arriving, for the first time, on the shores of the sea and then settling there. He envisions their first encounter with it: the unknown sounds, the beating winds, the new, exciting smells, and the urge to keep going despite the alarming newness of it all. And then, pushing aside the last branches, the opening of an incredible vista before their wondering eyes: "Before them lies the boundless lap of the sea, at once hostile and gentle, repellent and inviting, more mysterious than the forest, more homely than the starry sky, the end of one world and the beginning of another."[99] The opening pages of Meri's popular book also imagine a scene from the Viking age: a sentinel keeping nightwatch on the shore sees a fire lit on a nearby island, and quickly lights his own, to be followed by the next two – an ancient chain of shoreline bonfires to raise the alarm of foreign ships making a hostile approach.

---

[97] Jaak Haud Anto Raukas, Vello Salo and Peep Varju, *Eesti okupatsioonikahjud ja inimkaotused* (Tallinn: Valge Raamat, 2018), 67–82.
[98] Lennart Meri, *Hõbevalge* (Tallinn: Eesti Raamat, 1967), 9.   [99] Meri, 9.

*Environment and Society in Soviet Estonia* 33

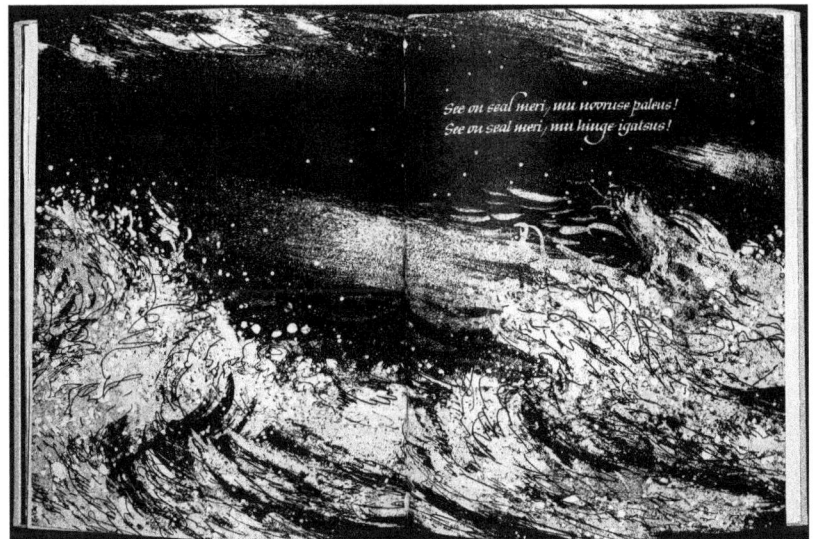

**Figure 13** From: Friedebert Tuglas, Meri. Tallinn: Eesti Raamat, 1966. Illustrated by Evald Okas.

In 1966, a year before the appearance of Meri's book, Friedebert Tuglas's epic poem *Meri* [*The Sea*, 1906] was re-issued in a deluxe edition, richly illustrated by Evald Okas, verses written in calligraphy by Villu Toots, in celebration of Tuglas's 80th birthday (Figure 13). The poem starts with lines, "How, as a child, I longed for the limitless sea."[100] The poetic persona in Tuglas's epic has been imprisoned by the Tsarist regime, and he looks to the sea from the window of his cell. In the next section we'll see how Lydia Koidula's poem *My Fatherland Is my Love* (1867) culminates with the poet's longing to become one with the homely soil after death – Tuglas ends his poem with a fantasy that his heart and life might merge with the sea. The poet dreams of having become a sea wave, roaring upon the shores of his homeland.[101]

Tuglas's introduction to this richly illustrated volume ends with a naked declaration: "And the sentiments expressed here [in the poem] still captivate me now."[102] Tuglas, then an old man, had written his canonical texts in the pre-Soviet decades, had been repressed in the Stalin era, and had regained in the post-Stalin years his eminent position as a living classic and a great connoisseur of pre-Soviet Estonian culture. His declaration invited readers to draw parallels between Tsarist rule and the Soviet era, and his poem anchored the parallels between these eras in the image of the sea as a symbol of unattainable freedom.

---

[100] Friedebert Tuglas, *Meri* (Tallinn: Eesti Raamat, 1966), 13. For some reason, as a child or as a teen, I was very much drawn to this book.
[101] Tuglas, 35.   [102] Tuglas, 11.

## Offending Cultural Expectations: The Militarized Sea

Access to the sea, this symbol of freedom and a defining figure in Estonians' cultural landscape, was restricted in the Soviet era by a dense network of prohibitions. The militarized landscape along Estonian coastal areas included "observation posts, missile bases, coastal defence batteries, trenches, observation towers, barracks, bunkers, border-guard stations, airfields, radar stations, commando points and army campuses, etc"[103] (Figures 14, 15). Jüri Pärn's provides a detailed description:

**Figures 14–15** One restricted zone during the Soviet era: the Soviet Submarine Degaussing Base near Hara. 2023. Photos by Anneli Leinpere.

---

[103] Miller, "Keep out! No Entry! Exploring the Soviet Military Landscape of the Coast of Estonia," 2.

**Figures 14–15** (cont.)

Along the coastal border, each BG [Border Guard] station had 2–10 posts consisting of up to 10 buildings and other constructions, where a detachment of 2–4 border guards would permanently or periodically be on duty. These posts consisted of technical surveillance posts with 1 or 2 stationary radars, a diesel power station, an observation tower and a searchlight mounted on rails; radiolocation posts with a small 1- or 2-storey building for the operation of a portable miniature radar; and mobile searchlight positions for coastline observation at night.[104]

Notwithstanding the presence of a vast military and border-guard machinery in Soviet Estonia, encounters with border troops and the refusals they issued often

---

[104] Jüri Pärn, "Soviet Military Infrastructure and Its Formation in Estonia," in *The Estonian Green Belt*, ed. Kalev Sepp (Tallinn: The Estonian University of Life Sciences, 2011), 26.

came as a surprise to the locals. Descriptions found in life-writings and oral testimonies abound with the surprise, disappointment, fear, and humiliation that typically accompanied these encounters. Often enough, the border zone was not marked as such with barbed wire or any other clearly identifiable sign, and – multiplying the occasions for misunderstanding – there were public beaches and vacation areas where access was granted until 10 pm in the evening. Regulations were not publicly posted and, when rules were changed, the only notice given was in brief announcements published in the local media. These rule changes typically related merely to changes in administrative divisions; Indrek Paavle has compared different regulations that governed border control over the Soviet decades and has concluded that "there were no fundamental changes in the system."[105]

Given the unavailability of reliable maps, accidental (or semi-accidental) crossings into restricted zones were bound to happen. In the absence of signage, how were hikers in the woods to know that they had trespassed into a border zone? The historian Indrek Paavle recollected his own experience from the mid-1980s, when he and his friends were hiking in the woods, only to be arrested by border troops; they were taken to the check point, their backpacks were thoroughly searched, and their interrogation lasted until morning – a situation the historian drily observed as "not among the most agreeable memories."[106] Similarly, the environmentalist Jaan Eilart shared how, when he was collecting data for a vegetation map, he heard the shouted demand "Hands up!" Eilart later told a journalist (possibly with some exaggeration) that he was forced to walk 5 kilometers, hands aloft the whole time, to a military base, where he was kept until the next day.[107] True, in November 1944, the composer and conductor Alfred Karindi (later arrested after the 1947 song festival) had it worse: when Karindi went to fetch milk from a neighboring farm, this everyday errand ended with his arrest: the locals had not been informed that the seaside was now considered a prohibited-access border zone. Karindi was arrested for illegal border crossing, he was taken to Tallinn, and, according to Aigi Rahi-Tamm's archival research, "it was made clear to him that he would be released only if he agreed to collaborate with the secret police. He received the agent name "Hope" and signed the papers but renounced the deal five years later."[108]

---

[105] Paavle, "Kuidas ära hoida 'nõukogudevastaste elementide karistamatu lahkumine'," 88.
[106] Paavle, 85.
[107] Katrin Pauts, "Jaan Eilarti elu meeldejäävaim jaanipäev – Äkki röögatas keegi selja taga: 'Käed üles!,'" *Õhtuleht*, June 21, 2001.
[108] Aigi Rahi-Tamm, "'Conflicts Are the Core of Social Life': Fomenting Mistrust at the Tallinn State Conservatory in the 1940s–60s," in *The Secret Police and the Soviet System: New Archival Investigations*, ed. Michael David-Fox (Pittsburgh: Pittsburgh University Press, 2023), 197–198.

**Figure 16** My only childhood visit to the Estonian islands: our family has acquired the necessary permit to visit friends on Hiiumaa island in the late 1970s. Photo by Arno Annus.

After a decade and more of Soviet rule, local people, now holders of special permits, had come to a clearer understanding of what was allowed and what not, and how to avoid or evade trouble. Border troops became part of the local social landscape, and, when necessary, they might have even lent a hand with work on the kolkhoz. Locals also ventured to visit beaches where access was officially prohibited – on Hiiumaa Island, as it seems, locals were simply asked to leave when caught by a patrol (Figure 16).[109] Yet already before the Soviet annexation, in the period of the interwar Republic, vacationing in the countryside and by the sea had been adopted by city dwellers as a summertime practice associated with a certain social prestige and cultural value.[110] When vacation-culture revived again after the war, in the 1950s, these "summer people" became especially exposed to trouble with the border troops, as they now and again found themselves on the wrong side of the border zone.

Here is one example, as narrated in 2014 by Toomas Haug as a free reconstruction of a child's perspective:

---

[109] Koppel, *Hiiumaa piiritsoon 1940–41 ja 1944–91*, 30. Miller, "Keep out! No Entry! Exploring the Soviet Military Landscape of the Coast of Estonia," 6.
[110] Kuusk and Kärginen, *Stopp! Piiritsoon*, 15.

> The long-awaited summer arrived at last and we eagerly travelled to Salmistu, where my mother's friends were vacationing in an old farmhouse, and near the site of one of the world's best sunbathing beaches.
>
> Of course, we knew that we were going to the border zone, and for that, we needed a *propusk*, a permit. But neither we nor our companions […] had a *propusk*. I remember that the kids were even a little worried about it. Our parents, however, were young people; they laughed at the funny word and thought: what could the border troops possibly do? It's summer, after all, and they'll surely understand that no one is going to swim to Finland. Secure in this belief, we all lounged on the sandy shore, on the beautiful beach of Salmistu. I, too, dutifully lay myself face down on a beach towel and blew sand into little hollows with my nose when, from the corner of my eye, I saw them coming: two soldiers, slowly wading across the sand, bulky rifles on their shoulders. Of course, they demanded that we present our *propusk*.[111]

The border troops marched the vacationers back to the station. One of the group members had thoughtlessly neglected to take his passport to the beach and was detained, while the others were permitted to return to their friend's farmhouse. Decades later, Haug still remembered his fear and the concern of the grown-up company, and how, disappointed and dispirited, they drove back to town in the evening. What would be the point in staying if people weren't allowed to enjoy the seashore?

Haug then continues with another recollection about another interaction with "soldiers": this time, the family had acquired the necessary *propusk* and had arrived upon the island of Saaremaa, where, upon disembarking, the border guards would check everyone's documents. "Saaremaa was like a fairytale land, guarded by an evil witch and difficult to access," comments the author, reproducing his recollection of a child's-eye perspective.[112]

Even as "the evil witch" thwarted access to the holiday sites of one's dreams, the seaside remained an appealing summer destination. The sense and feel of the seashore, especially in combination with the simplicity of countryside life, was figured as a restorative and revitalizing force. While the Khrushchev era had initiated a boom of summer home construction, summer vacation on a pre-Soviet farm home was widely considered a more authentic way to spend one's vacation time.[113] Media and fictional works reflected and consolidated such visions.

---

[111] Haug, *Mööda Koidu tänavat*, 61. [112] Haug, 63.
[113] Epp Annus, *Soviet Postcolonial Studies: A View from the Western Borderlands* (London: Routledge, 2018); Epp Annus, "Maakodu Eesti NSV-S. Kultuurilised kujutelmad ja argised asjad," *Keel ja Kirjandus*, no. 6 (2019): 425–40; Epp Annus, "Comparative Spatial Intimacies and the Affective Geography of Home: Imaginaries and Sense-Regimes in the Soviet-Era Baltics," *Space and Culture* (2023): 1–16; Epp Lankots and Triin Ojari, eds., *Leisure Spaces. Holiday and Architecture in 20th Century Estonia* (Tallinn: Estonian Museum of Architecture, 2020).

Take Jaan Kruusvall's short story *Sortsi leib* [*Sorcerer's Bread*, 1973]: Antu, a young man, spends weeks in a quiet seashore village, in a semi-dilapidated house recently purchased by his sister. Antu keeps himself as detached as possible from modern life. He doesn't have a radio or newspaper; he lays on the beach, swims, tramps about, climbs the church tower, and sometimes helps an elderly relative with farm work. In time, he becomes altogether caught up into the local environment, and with the sea, above all:

> He turned over onto his back. Waves washed over him, and he could taste the saltwater in his mouth. Spitting it out, he felt the vast sea rocking beneath his body; he could feel the breathing and the power of the ocean. It was an unthinkable immensity of water. Then he dove several meters to the bottom. As he swam along the seabed, he felt the caress of seaweed across his belly. A large turbot flashed past him like lightning.[114]

There by the sea, disconnected from the city and modern urban life, "he feels, at last, as if he were his own true self."[115]

The "nature therapy" that restores Antu to his authentic wholeness performs its magic in quiet surroundings and relative seclusion. In its ideal, a deep sense of unity with the surrounding natural environment was figured as attainable as a solitary or semi-solitary affair. A 1972 painting, *A Man Listening to the Sea*, by Aili Vint (Figure 17), visualizes this ideal: the man on the sand has blended with the sand and the sand has blended with the sea, each color and each natural substance – the sandy seashore, the sea, the sky – reflecting back others, all together forming a harmonious, quiet, open-ended unity of the world, with no sign of any human-made structures or social presence in sight.

The imaginary of finding harmony in nature, figured over and against modernity and urban life, was hardly an Estonian invention, of course. Indeed we can see that Antu's figure belongs to the general context of a partial disillusionment with industrial, urbanized late modernity between the late 1960s and the mid-1980s – a disillusionment that motivated a turn toward alternatives in both nature and history.[116]

Antu's nature-oriented self-realization may prompt comparisons with rural visions in Russian "Village Prose," a prominent Russian literary movement of the same era. Yet Russian authors Valentin Rasputin, Aleksandr Solzhenitsyn, and others lamented the lost simplicity and virtue of village life, replaced by the spiritually debasing forces of urbanization and industrialization – a precise cast

---

[114] Jaan Kruusvall, *Armastuse esimene pool* (Tallinn: Eesti Raamat, 1973), 77.
[115] Kruusvall, 86.
[116] Denis Kozlov, "The Historical Turn in Late Soviet Culture: Retrospectivism, Factography, Doubt, 1953–91," *Kritika: Explorations in Russian and Eurasian History* 2, no. 3 (2001): 577–600.

**Figure 17** Aili Vint. A man listening to the sea. 1972. Oil on canvas. Art Museum of Estonia.

of sentiment that was lacking in Estonian fiction.[117] In Estonian culture, by that time, visions of a harmonious co-existence with nature were typically accompanied by an acknowledgment of the city and its life as a place of return.

## Conclusion: Regimes at Variance: Dreams of the Sensuous Earth and the Hard Power of Colonial Policing

In the border regions of the Soviet Union, such as in the Estonian SSR, but also in the Latvian and Lithuanian SSRs (notwithstanding Lithuania's comparatively limited shoreline), dreams of a communion with nature ran headlong into the obstacles of a restrictive border regime. The very visible presence of armed Soviet military and border troops in the Estonian SSR significantly impinged upon eco-social relations of the era. Limited access to the seashore and

---

[117] Geoffrey A Hosking, "The Russian Peasant Rediscovered: 'Village Prose' of the 1960s," *Slavic Review* 32, no. 4 (1973): 705–24; Kathleen F Parthé, *Russian Village Prose: The Radiant Past* (Princeton: Princeton University Press, 1992).

document spot-checks at the unlikeliest of outdoor activities, common as they were, were experienced as intrusions into "our right" to be in "our land" – a version of colonial eco-social violence.

Perhaps the defining feature of this form of state violence was its utter absurdity from the perspective of those involved on the local side – to them, it was self-evident that vacationers at the beach were not contemplating an escape across the sea. Their expectation was to leave behind the demands and pressures of quotidian life, to lay immobile on the shore, to blow small pits in the sand through the breath of their nostrils, to dive into the sea and sense how the coolness of the water embraces the body, to feel the heat of the sun on the skin and to run into the water again to cool off. The interventions of armed border troops thus created an absurd, disruptive, and dismaying incongruity between the hard force of colonial-style policing and the very different realm of the sensuous earth, the sea, the sand, the fresh breeze from across the sea, the rocks on the shores.

Of the hundreds of border troop stories that I have heard or read, perhaps the most memorable concerns a dead cow. The cow died on the tiny Vilsandi island (Figure 18), because the veterinarian was delayed by official restrictions upon movement in the border zone. Ordinary visitors had to "first apply for a permit at their passport office in their place of residence, then register themselves at the border guard headquarters in the town of Kuressaare on the larger island of

**Figure 18** Cows on Vilsandi Island in 1930, before the Soviet era. National Archives of Estonia, EFA.554.0.185710. Unknown photographer.

Saaremaa, and finally again make themselves known at the Kihelkonna outpost."[118]

This story, narrated by Tormis Jakovlev, was told to him by residents of Saaremaa, who reported both the fact of the cow's death and their sense that compensation was later obtained for its untimely demise. Compensation, of course, may or may not have satisfied the owner, but it could not change the sad fate of the cow in question. The cow, of course, had not chosen where to live; nonetheless, it fell victim to the border zone regulations.

Somehow this story has stuck with me. Countless stories of border troops, told in retrospect and without mentioning dates, focus on affect: fear, disappointment, the sense of offense, the ridicule. The story of the cow scarcely goes beyond its mere fact; it is practically an image rather than a story, yet the image of the big dead carcass on a scarcely inhabited island strikes an existential note. Remote from political struggle, a cow dies on a rocky, wind-swept island, because of an absurdly strict border regime in the Baltic borderlands of the USSR: a powerful image of excessive colonial violence leaving victims both human and nonhuman.

The common and widely circulated narratives of locals encountering armed Russian-speaking border troops contributed significantly to the oppressive sense of Russian control over Estonia. Even as these guards hailed from different parts of the Soviet Union, for the local people they all, indifferently, signified "Russian rule," as Soviet rule was generally called. I have elsewhere explained this as structural question:

> No matter what their personal convictions were, they [the border guards] now started to function as part of an oppressive power structure: they surveilled the seashores, raked sand to expose future foot traffic, searched over the surface of the sea with powerful spotlights, and restricted movement in the areas close to the Soviet border, all while interacting with the locals in the Russian language.[119]

For the locals, the incongruity between the sensuous earth and the excessive colonial order fostered an internal protest, a discord, and resentment.

*Often, if not every day, my mother and I, in the summers of the 1970s and 1980s, would encounter border troops marching along our road, as we walked between our summer home and our local public beach, not far from Tallinn. They marched that road daily, as we knew – perhaps even several times per day. Later in the evening, we could see their vehicle making its patrol along the beach. As we walked under the pine trees, anticipating the deeply pleasant juxtaposition of cool water and dry, hot sun and sand, these face-to-face*

---

[118] Tormis Jakovlev, "Nõukogude armee Lääne-Saaremaal ja selle suhted kohalike elanikega," 1998, www.saaremaa.ee/index.php?option=com_content&view=article&id=136%0A.

[119] Annus, *Soviet Postcolonial Studies: A View from the Western Borderlands*, 184.

*encounters with armed men in uniform presented a violent incongruity, a disruption of mood carrying an element of reflexive fear.*

*This summer I again spent some weeks at our summer home. The border troop barracks have by now been renovated into private homes. I no longer go to the beach in mid-day or in the early afternoon – it's too hot. The climate in Estonia and northern Europe has warmed at a rate faster than the global average. Yet I start my day every morning with this same walk, the warmth of sleep hastening my steps in anticipation of the coolness of the water. The beach is nearly empty at this early hour. The pine trees have grown.*

*Every morning, I venture into the water in exactly the same spot as in my childhood, stepping into the sea between the two biggest rocks, one of them folded low in middle – the erratic boulders pushed here from Scandinavia at the end of the ice-age, together with the receding ice. Close to one of my rocks is another, hidden under the surface of the water, but I know where it is. I pass it, and then it's time to swim out to the open sea.*

## 3 The Sound of the Choir Is the Sound of the Earth: The Song, the Land, the Nation, and Decolonization. 1969, 1869, 1988

"The year 1968 began in hope and ended in disillusion," in Ronald Suny's blunt assessment.[120] Both locally and globally, the Soviet-led invasion of Czechoslovakia on August 21 was understood as the end of the partial liberalization that had gained ground across the Soviet bloc since the death of Stalin. In Estonia, in October 1968, the last of the Tartu University students' legendary 1960s torch-lit parades ended in arrests.[121] After two years of dispute, Paul-Eerik Rummo's existentialist play *Tuhkatriinumäng* [*The Cinderella Game*] was finally greenlit for staging at the Vanemuine theatre in Tartu – this victory, however, was followed by bans upon several subsequent theatre projects. Rummo, the most promising Estonian poet of the 1960s, had become caught up in the censorship apparatus and did not publish a single book throughout the 1970s.[122] The important cultural broadsheet, *Sirp ja Vasar*, engaged in a debate over existentialism in Estonian prose: wasn't there a case to be made, after all, that literary expressions of anxiety and absurdity betrayed Soviet values? Existentialist undertones undeniably permeated the 1960s Estonian cultural sphere, supported by translations of classic existentialist works: Albert

---

[120] Ronald Grigor Suny, ed., *The Structure of Soviet History: Essays and Documents* (New York: Oxford University Press, 2003), 388.
[121] Jaak Allik, "Jaak Allik jätkab vastamist," *Teater. Muusika. Kino*, no. 10 (1991): 68; Eleri Vako, "' Meie aeg lööb auku müüri'. 1968. aasta üliõpilaspäevad Tartus ja Tallinnas," *Akadeemia*, no. 2 (2008): 411–61.
[122] Epp Annus, *Sotskolonialism Eesti NSV-s. Võim, kultuur, argielu* (Tartu: Tartu Ülikooli Kirjastus, 2019), 137, 240–44.

**Figure 19** The 1969 Song Festival. Unknown photographer. Estonian Literary Museum, EKLA, B-114:94.

Camus's *La Peste* was published in Estonian translation in 1963, Franz Kafka's *Prozess* in 1966, Camus's *L'Étranger* in 1966 and Camus's *Le Mythe de Sisyphe* following in 1972. In Russian, the first translations of Camus's work were published a few years later, in 1968.[123]

Amid marked constrictions in the political and cultural space, preparations were in full swing for long-planned festivities to celebrate, in June 1969, the hundredth anniversary of the Estonian song festivals (Figure 19). The first major multi-day gathering of Estonian singers and musicians had taken place in Tartu, 1869, when 51 collectives with 878 male performers performed jointly to a crowd of about 15,000 listeners.[124] Since then, the song festival tradition had become a major event in Estonian culture, a mass gathering where national belonging was experienced in a direct, bodily-affective way.

The Soviet regime sanctioned the song festival tradition in hopes of appropriating it as an occasion for mass indoctrination. As a party official explained in 1950: "Soviet mass singing is among the best ways to engage the active

---

[123] Emily Tall, "Camus in the Soviet Union: Some Recent Emigrés Speak," *Comparative Literature Studies* 16, no. 3 (1979): 237–49.

[124] Rudolf Põldmäe, *Esimene Eesti Üldlaulupidu 1869* (Tallinn: Eesti Raamat, 1969).

involvement of the masses and to educate them in the spirit of communism and Soviet patriotism."[125] The 1947 song festival, the first after Soviet annexation, had turned into a national celebration despite the loss of independent statehood. After the arrest of its organizers, the explanation given was that

> Bourgeois nationalists Andresen, Semper, Vettik, Karindi, and Päts tried to give the song festival an apolitical character, to detach the repertoire from actual life [...]. These bourgeois nationalists continued their subversive activities even after the song festival: they also conspired to make the program of the 1950 song festival politically infertile and thus deprive the people of an important tool for their political education.[126]

The 1950 song festival was a strictly policed Stalinist event; after Stalin's death in 1953, however, the festivals regained some measure of their pre-Soviet sensibility. The programs offered space for political programming, but also for singing traditional pre-Soviet choral songs – songs that typically expressed feelings of national belonging through the affecting imagery of a beautiful homeland. These massive choral festivals, with tens of thousands of performers, were unique to the cultures of Estonia, Latvia, and Lithuania.

In the nineteenth century, the earliest song festivals cultivated and shaped Estonians' national self-awareness under Baltic-German and Russian double colonial rule.[127] Remarkably, song festivals were able to perform similar work in the twentieth century. The tradition rooted in German *Sängerfeste*, from the era of German unification, had traveled across time and place to serve as a platform for non-Soviet sentiment and to sustain a sense of cultural continuity, despite profound changes in political realities. In this sense, the imposition of Soviet rule froze in time certain cultural practices that might otherwise have faded away in the passing of generations.

### Celebration of Continuity: 1969. *Koit* [*The Dawn*]

In June 1969, accompanied by the singing of a male choir, the *laulupeotuli*, the symbolic flame of the song festival, was lit with the first rays of the sun in Tartu on the site of the first Estonian song festival in 1869. From this ritual beginning, the symbolic torch was then carried on its journey to the capital city of Tallinn, its

---

[125] Aleksander Kelberg, "Nõukogude Eesti 1950. a. üldlaulupidu," in *Nõukogude Eesti 1950. a. üldlaulupeo juht* (Tallinn: Eesti Riiklik Kirjastus, 1950), 8.
[126] Kelberg, 6.
[127] Nineteenth-century colonialism in this context was double-layered owing to the relative autonomy, within the Russian Empire, granted to the Baltic German nobility in the Governorates of Estonia and Livonia. Epp Annus, *Soviet Postcolonial Studies: A View from the Western Borderlands* (London: Routledge, 2018), chap. 5; Ea Jansen, *Vaateid Eesti rahvusluse sünniaegadesse* (Tartu: Ilmamaa, 2004).

**Figure 20** The eighth Estonian Song Festival, 1923. Unknown photographer. Estonian Literary Museum, EKLA, A-225:2832.

passage celebrated with concerts all along the way.[128] The two-week-long festivities culminated in celebrations that gathered over 30,000 performers from 771 music collectives and brought about 200,000 people to the festival grounds in Tallinn.

The anniversary structure of the 1969 jubilee celebration gave the organizers license to program a good number of songs from earlier, pre-Soviet festivals, and to dedicate the festival to the theme of continuity. The first festival concert in Tallinn that year, in late June, 1969, opened with *Koit* [*Dawn*], by Mihkel Lüdig, words by Friedrich Kuhlbars, a song that had its song festival premiere in 1923, the first festival of the independent Estonian Republic (Figure 20). In the nascent republic, this song resounded as the hymn of a new era – even though the song itself, written in 1904, predated the founding of the Estonian Republic.

*Koit* is a brief, musically intricate composition, crafted for seven voices, that celebrates the beauty of the homeland:

> Songs are now flowing as beautiful music,
> Crossing our country in powerful streams.
> Beauty is flourishing in verdant gardens:
> The earth of the Fatherland awakens to blossom and bloom.
> Dawn now glimmers high upon hilltops.
> Let the flame of our hopes rise to the sky![129]

---

[128] Arvo Ratassepp, *Eesti laulupeod* (Tallinn: Perioodika, 1985), 30–33.

[129] English translation: Guntis Šmidchens, *The Power of Song: Nonviolent National Culture in the Baltic Singing Revolution* (Seattle: University of Washington Press, 2014), 102. The translation has been altered.

As was common enough with the romantic national songs that flourished before the Great War, *Koit* celebrated the beauty of a fatherland suffused by song – here, lyric and melody and affect flow over the land like streams of water and the beautiful dawn awakens the land and human hope to their potential fulfilment. Within this vision, the beauty of the fatherland is naturally bound together with its human cultivation – if the hills are beautiful, so too are the verdant gardens. The land and its human cultivation are celebrated as a harmonious whole.

The romantic union of nature and culture was also highlighted in popular media coverage of the 1969 song festival. Indeed, the song celebration was described as if it offered a vision of culture and nature transcending human-nonhuman binaries: "The choirs on stage sang, the sea of people in the square sang, the trees in the park joined in, the limestone shore and the sea waves sang along,"[130] wrote the critic Oskar Kruus in the weekly *Sirp ja Vasar*.

Such powerful sentiments, experienced by tens of thousands, form a distinct strand among Estonian imaginaries of nature. Often, choral song, performed in open-air concerts, is figured as echoing and resounding together with the surrounding land and landscapes. One even finds a more-than-human characterization of song in festival contexts: song is not simply perceived as an art form for expressing human sentiments, but as human vocal cords giving voice to the land itself.

Singing in the context of the song festival, then, is not most profoundly grasped by festivalgoers as an expression of patriotism or even the sense of belonging together with one's people and their place. Song is a way to sound in unison with the land, earth, and sea (Figure 21). In the Estonian context, this vision has its roots in folklore. Take the famous Estonian folk song *Lauliku lapsepõli* [*A Singer's Childhood*], set to music by Miina Härma and performed at the 1969 festival: the lyric details how a child, a future singer, learns to sing from a bird and a duck, and later simply transcribes the song he'd heard issuing from the natural world. The first task of the singer is to listen and attend to the music of the world – this folkloric figure preceded the era of nation-building.

The connection of lyric to land was sometimes also figured as transcending mere locality to express and support a sense of existential or planetary belonging. Take the words of the beloved long-term conductor Gustav Ernesaks, who contemplated the powerful convergence of song, nation, and earth in his memoirs: "The sound of the grand choir is like the sound of the nation itself. A Sound of the Earth."[131] Ernesaks himself had come to symbolize national

---

[130] Oskar Kruus, "Ühte käisid meie hääled, ühte sündisid südamed," *Sirp ja Vasar*, July 4, 1969, 4.
[131] Gustav Ernesaks, *Kutse* (Tallinn: Eesti Raamat, 1980), 187.

**Figure 21** The sea, the sky, the trees, and the song festival grounds filled with people – the song festival experience as transcending mere national sentiment. 1960. Photographer Ingrid Rüütel. Estonian Literary Museum, EKLA, B-114:31.

continuity: as a 14-year-old, he had attended the 1923 song festival, in the independent interwar Estonian Republic – and he conducted his legendary song *Mu isamaa on minu arm* [*My fatherland is my love*] for the last time in 1990, when Estonia had reasserted its sovereignty[132] and the Soviet Union was disintegrating. When Ernesaks died three years later in 1993, it was in an independent Estonia.

### *My Fatherland Is My Love*? Cultural Hybridities and Finno-Ugrian Inspirations

The 1969 festival culminated with *Mu isamaa on minu arm* [*My fatherland is my love*], with words by Lydia Koidula and melody by Gustav Ernesaks, a much-loved song that over the Soviet years came to function as an unofficial national anthem – it being strictly forbidden to perform the actual national anthem of the former Estonian republic, and official Soviet anthems inspiring no popular affective response.

Koidula's poem was first published in 1867 and was written in a register typical of nineteenth-century romantic nationalism: the verses pair an intimate

---

[132] The Supreme Soviet of the Estonian SSR issued a Declaration of the Sovereignty of the Estonian SSR and the supremacy of its own laws over those of the USSR on November 16, 1988.

declaration of love for one's homeland with a hymnic proclamation of one's readiness to die for it. The piece ends with an expression of lyrical longing for a final repose in the lap of the poet's homeland:[133]

> My fatherland is my love
> To whom I gave my heart,
> I sing to you, my greatest joy,
> My blossoming Estonia!
> […]
> My fatherland is my love,
> And I want to rest;
> Upon your lap I fall asleep,
> My sacred Estonia!
> Your birds now sing me to sleep,
> You grow flowers from my remains
> My fatherland![134]

Koidula was not only a beloved poet – she had also taken an active role in organizing the first song festival in 1869. Moreover, her lyrics *Mu isamaa on minu arm* [*My fatherland is my love*] and *Sind surmani* [*You Until Death*], having been set to music by Aleksander Kunileid, were the only original Estonian songs included in the program for that first festival – other inclusions having been adapted from German originals.[135] By all accounts, *Mu isamaa on minu arm* was one of the highlights of the 1869 festival: participants remarked on its powerful romantic pathos of commitment, expressed in intimate, conversational 'thou'-form. The body-to-body congruence – the linkage of homeland and the poet's body in deep intimacy, the flowers of her homeland springing forth from her dead body – these images offered an eco-intimate figure for binding both poetic persona and national belonging to the natural world.

*Mu isamaa on minu arm*, with Ernesaks's newly composed musical setting, was performed with great success in the early postwar years. With the tightening of Stalinist control, it was banned from the official concert repertoire until it could return in the political and cultural thaw of the 1960s.

---

[133] Lydia Koidula, *Emmajöe Öpik. I.* (Tartu: H. Laakmann, 1867), 29.

[134] The Estonian language does not have a future tense. Translators of this lyric, spooked perhaps by the strangeness of Koidula's imagery in the last stanza, have typically translated it into the English future. I have taken the liberty here to restore it to its clear (if strange) present sense.

[135] Most songs sung at the first Estonian and Latvian festivals were based on German melodies, their words often adaptations of German songs. Homi Bhabha calls such empowering mirroring "colonial specularity": The word "fatherland" had, for Germans, referred to Germany, yet by an easy gesture of appropriation it was now repurposed for Estonian nation-building. Homi K. Bhabha, *The Location of Culture* (London: Routledge, 1994), 114. See also Annus, *Soviet Postcolonial Studies: A View from the Western Borderlands*, 147–48.

Koidula's verses, with their vision of a nationally attuned eco-intimacy, cast her poet into an embrace with her homeland. Yet the story of the cultural trajectory of this lyric complicates this vision: indeed, the story suggests the way Estonian culture has been constellated from transnational points of reference. The original version of Koidula's song premiered in St Petersburg and was first performed by a Germanophone choir. Ernesaks composed his new musical setting for Koidula's lyric in March 1944 in Leningrad (formerly St Petersburg), where it too had its premiere.[136] When, in 1873, Koidula finally married, it was to Eduard Michelson, a Latvian by birth and German by cultural upbringing – after which she spent much of the rest of her life in Kronstadt, a fortified island town west of St. Petersburg, and this, in fact, was where she died.

Koidula's flesh having joined the land in Kronstadt, her bones were transferred in 1946 to Estonia and reburied there, a gesture that testified to Koidula's poetic witness, but also to persisting postwar fantasies of an ethnic determination of homeland. Later, in the 1980s, the circumstances and events around Koidula's reburial gave material for the writer Mati Unt who fictionalized them in a drama and an ironic postmodern novel.[137] The "actual" story of Koidula's song, and the story of Estonian culture more generally, was not about a bodily intertwining of poetic self and homeland: it was the story of accidents and exiles and cultural crisscrossings.

The cultural constellation of history is manifest likewise in a famous series of graphic works by Kaljo Põllu, dated to the same year 1969 and dedicated to the hundredth anniversary of the song festival tradition (Figures 22–24). The motif of a young woman in folk costume is repeatedly stereotyped in blue across the bottom of each of the black and white graphic works in the series, thus staging the typically forbidden arrangement of the blue-black-white of the Estonian pre-Soviet tricolor. The central imagery on each scene varies from a traditional farm dwelling, to a feminized archetypal southern Estonian landscape, to a church surrounded by trees, to a massive sacral oak tree – producing a series which, according to a 1971 commentator, "unveils the mental world" of the ancestors.[138] This mental world is constituted, in Põllu's vision, by a collage of homely landscapes, pre-Christian sacrality, farm settings, and the Lutheran church.

In the 1970s, Põllu would explore 'the mental world of the ancestors' within a rather different framing: drawing inspiration from expeditions organized by Tartu linguists and ethnographers, he launched what became a tradition of

---

[136] Paul Rummo, "Ühe laulu lugu," *Looming*, no. 1 (1961): 111–28.

[137] Epp Annus, "Neoliberalism or Postmodernism? Decolonizing Soviet Estonia, 1987–1991," *Journal of Baltic Studies*, September (2024), 1–20.

[138] Tiina Nurk, "Kaljo Põllu," in *Kaljo Põllu*, ed. Tiina Nurk (Tallinn; Tartu: Eesti NSV Kultuuriministeerium, Tartu Riiklik Kunstimuuseum, 1972), 5.

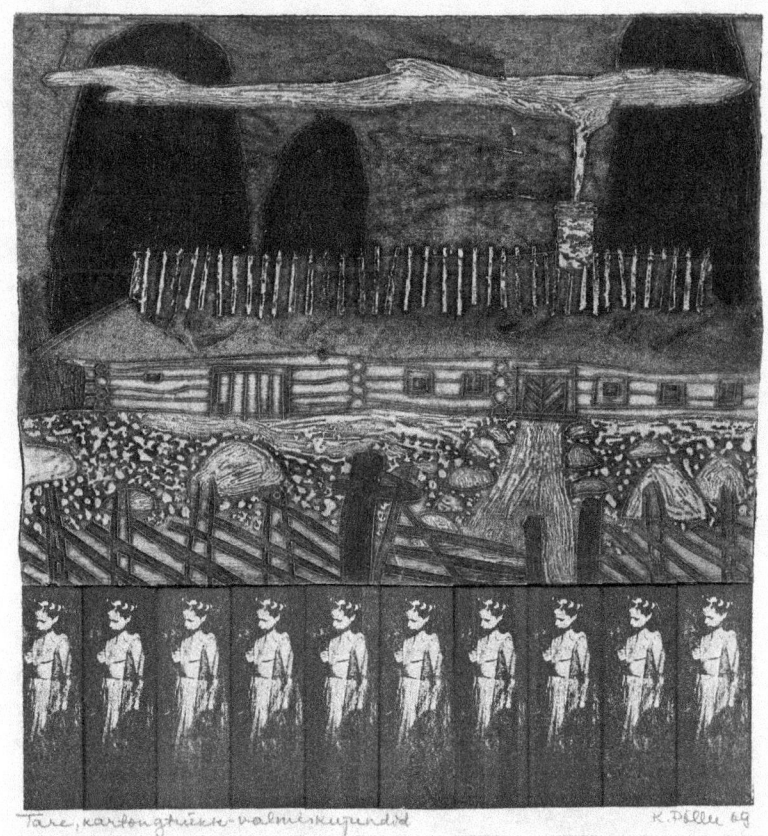

**Figures 22–24** Kaljo Põllu. A Farm Dwelling. From the edge of the cloud. Bells. 1969. Cardboard print, ready-made shapes, cliché. Art Museum of Estonia.

ethnographic art expeditions to different Finno-Ugric peoples that would last until 2017: in 1978, he led the first group of art students to the Kola Peninsula to visit the Sámi people.[139] In this, Põllu was part of a cultural movement that found inspiration in a vision of the common cultural roots of Finno-Ugric peoples: in 1969, Lennart Meri started shooting his *Veelinnurahvas* [*The Waterfowl People*, 1970], followed by the Estonian-Finnish co-production of *Linnutee tuuled* [*The Winds of the Milky Way*, 1977] – both films documented the everyday lives of different Finno-Ugric and Samoyedic peoples. The composer Veljo Tormis found inspiration in Estonian, but also in other Finno-Ugric

---

[139] Marika Alver, "Eesti Kunstiakadeemia 40 soome-ugri ekspeditsiooni (1978–2017): Sisemine järjepidevus ja paradigmamuutused," *Eesti Rahva Muuseumi aastaraamat* 63, no. 2 (2021): 177–210.

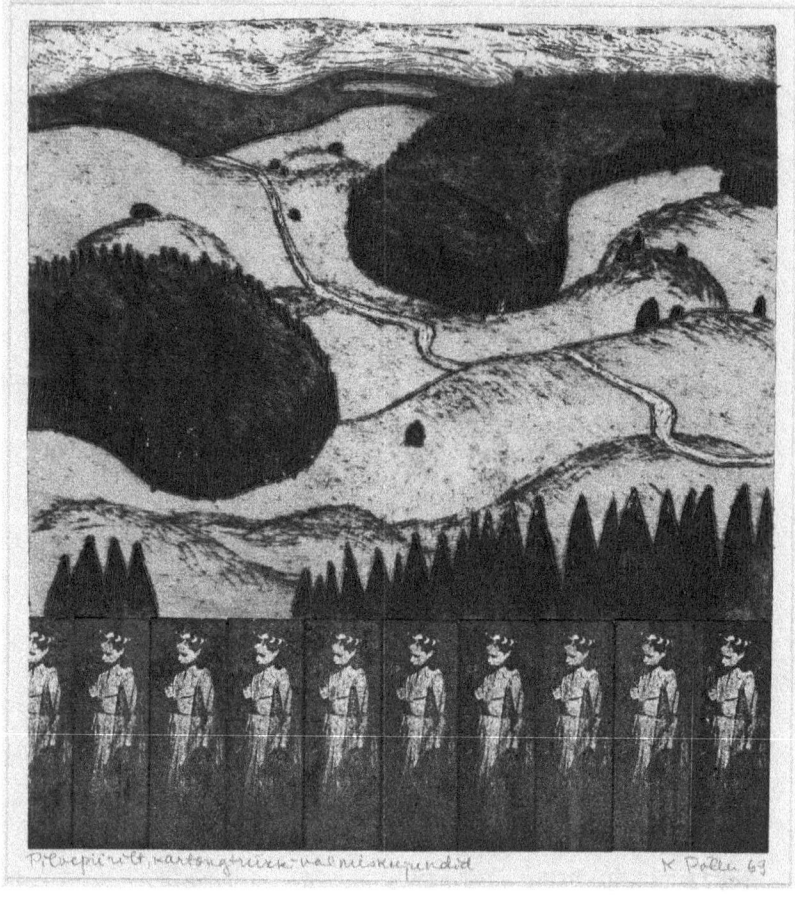

**Figures 22–24** (cont.)

folk traditions; his famous cycle of choral works, written in the 1970s and 1980s, *Unustatud rahvad* [*Forgotten Peoples*], made use of Livonian, Votic, Ingrian, Veps, and Karelian folk tunes. In 1969, Tormis accompanied the Nature Conservation Society's expedition to Livonian villages, a journey that inspired the first part of his cycle. His cycle opens with the Livonian folk song "Waking the Birds" – a song that Livonian youth presumably once sang, in the past, on the shores of the Baltic Sea, to rouse the birds from their slumber and call them to their labors.

All these expeditionary and archival explorations were drawn to the poetics of a common Finno-Ugric ancestry, to a vision that nature-oriented archaic traditions, discernible still in some Finno-Ugric cultures, would provide inspiration for new creative work.

*Environment and Society in Soviet Estonia* 53

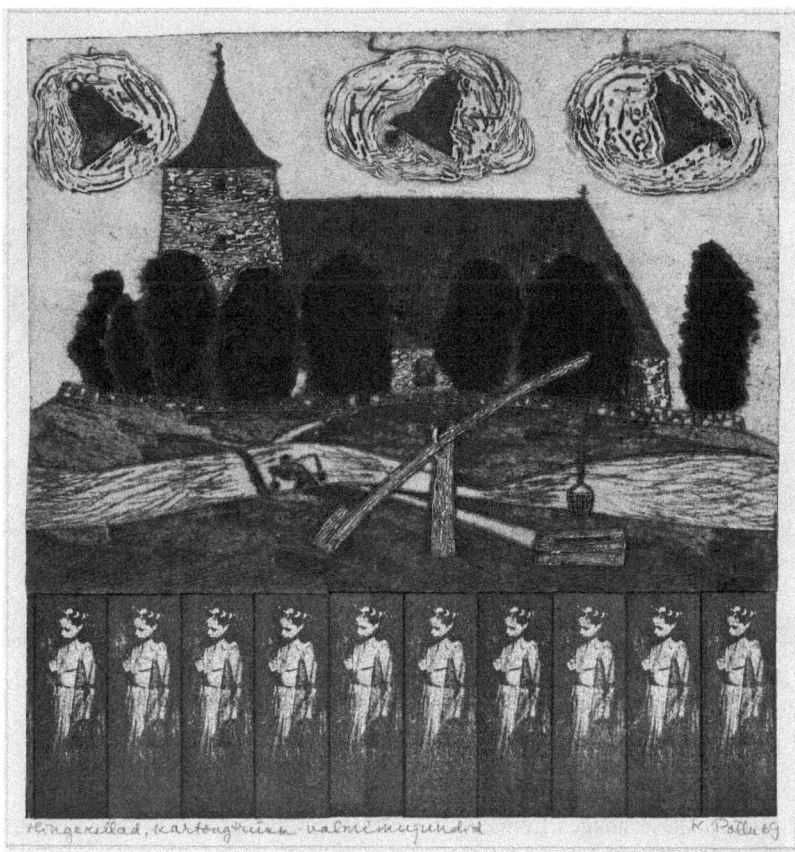

**Figures 22–24** (cont.).

## The First Singers Were the Wind and the Waves

For the song-festival centennial celebration in 1969, print culture also contributed a monograph about the first Estonian song festival and a richly illustrated album *Laulusajand 1869–1969* [*A Century of Song 1869–1969*].[140] The album's poetic presentation of the festival tradition, in images and narrative, effectively reinforced the assemblage of song, land, and nation.

*Laulusajand* opens with several pages of images: landscapes, clouds, water, birds, plants, and insects are offered to readers without any text to justify their role in an album celebrating a century of choral song festivals. With their up-to-date technique and their distinctive 1960s aesthetic, the photographs show every sign of having been taken in the years just prior to the centenary itself – and yet,

---

[140] Põldmäe, *Esimene Eesti üldlaulupidu 1869*; Valdo Pant, *Laulusajand 1869–1969*, ed. Aarne Mesikäpp, Valdo Pant, and Aron Tamarkin (Tallinn: Eesti Raamat, 1969).

**Figure 25** An image from the album Laulusajand 1869–1969. Tallinn: Eesti Raamat, 1969. Unknown photographer.

strikingly, these images from Soviet-era Estonia conspicuously lack even the least visible sign of Soviet rule (Figure 25). The first full-page panoramic image draws the readers' glance over forests, fields and traditional farm homes scattered across the landscape. On the facing page, four smaller images present a cloudy sky, a dense forest of tall fir trees, a close-up of the sea with small waves lapping the rocks near shore, and a field of grain bounded at the rear by a line of fir trees. Each of these is an archetypal image of Estonianness; in combination, they suggest a certain inviolability of the land entirely apart from the comings and goings of political rules and regimes. We find, on the next page, seated with a harp on his lap, the figure of Vanemuine, putative pagan god of music (in fact a neo-mythological device invented by nineteenth-century Estonian Romantics). The graphic imprint of Vanemuine is set against the backdrop of yet another Estonian countryside landscape, this time the picturesque image of a traditional lakeside farm home. Together, they compose a collage-like double-layered image in which the landscape shimmers faintly through the body of the "ancient god." The pages that follow present more of the same: images of birds, plants, and insects, the close-up of a nineteenth-century farmstead – all, again, photographed according to the conventions of modern aesthetics, where the image of the main

**Figure 26a,b** An image from the album Laulusajand 1869–1969. Unknown photographer.

building is bounded on the right by the log wall of another very close to the camera and where the forest treetops are seen peaking at the camera from behind the farmhouse (Figure 26). Still, markers of Soviet regime are nowhere to be seen.

After nine pages of pure imagery, the album finally offers readers two familiar lines of text from Koidula's lyric, *Mu isamaa on minu arm*: "My fatherland is my love / to whom I have given my heart ... ", as an epigraph to what then develops as an autochthonous story of creation, in which the tale of the nation is composed by braiding together images of nature, ancient traditions, and the birth of song:

> The first singers were the wind and the waves. There is something of the pine tree in the wind and something of the rocks by the sea in us. [...]
> Then Vanemuine sang. [...]
> Then the mother sang by her cradle. The spinning wheel whirred, the sparkle of light flickered in the hut and the night crept behind the window.
> Everything started from here.[141]

Readers are presented with a poetic tale of the autochthonous births of song, a singing tradition, and the whole of a nation – all, as it would seem, springing forth from the winds and the waves, the pines and the rocky shores, drawing from the energies of the Earth and setting it all amid the timeless cycle of lives and deaths – a story strikingly different, indeed worlds apart, from the typical Soviet historical narrative of class struggle in its march toward the inevitable victory of communism. Here, the anti-colonial gesture figures Estonianness as rooted in nature and part and parcel

---

[141] Pant, *Laulusajand 1869–1969*.

with the singing tradition, indeed with song itself, something so ancient that a few decades of rule, one way or another, will leave only a passing trace on its body of forests, lakes, seas, and traditional dwellings. Mythic fantasy and the poetic imaginary frame a world and a people purged of contemporary historical reality.

In the context of a highly ideologized Soviet print culture, the *Laulusajand* album was a striking publication in many respects, but it was emblematic of the special character of the 1969 song festival: it visualized temporal parallels between past and present, and poeticized the pre-Soviet past through nature imagery. Even more remarkably, the album managed to skirt many of the otherwise obligatory narrative strategies and commonplaces of the Soviet era. Under Soviet rule in the Baltics, print culture was heavily regulated and censored. Local publications had to reproduce pregiven models in their presentation of historical processes: "acceptable" models were introduced from Soviet Russia and then disseminated through ideological texts translated from Russian and through other forms of political education. Vernacular modern histories were recomposed as histories of class struggle, highlighting both a vilification of the preceding period of independence (as a "dictatorship of the bourgeoisie") and a special new emphasis on "historical friendships with the Russian people."[142] The introduction to a book about the history of Estonian song festivals, published just a few years before the centenary, stressed its aim of giving a "Marxist interpretation to Estonian song festivals" and diligently reproduced the canonical mode of writing about such things: it adopted a strongly pejorative tone in its survey of festivals prior to the advent of the Soviet takeover, upon which, at long last, the people were finally free to "sing about matters close to their hearts: about their bright lives, about their leader in the struggle – the Communist Party."[143] In the Estonian SSR, these more strictly policed modes of writing about the pre-Soviet past began to relax – and then only slowly – in the 1970s.[144]

---

[142] Epp Annus, "The Colonizer's Day off: Colonial Subjectivities in the Soviet-Era Baltics," in *Postcolonialism and Its New Discontents: Envisioning New Relations to the Colonial Past*, ed. Monika Albrecht (London: Routledge, 2019), 240–54; Vita Gruodytė, "Lithuanian Musicology in Historical Context: 1945 to the Present," *Journal of Baltic Studies* 39, no. 3 (2008): 263–82; Kevin C Karnes, "Soviet Musicology and the 'Nationalities Question': The Case of Latvia," *Journal of Baltic Studies* 39, no. 3 (2008): 283–305.

[143] Aron Tamarkin, ed., *Lauluga läbi aegade* (Tallinn: Eesti Raamat, 1965), 5.

[144] Virve Sarapik, "How to Write Soviet Estonian Art History: Three Attempts, from Stalinism through the Khrushchev Thaw and Beyond," *Kunstiteaduslikke Uurimusi* 24, no. 3/4 (2015): 150–72.

## From Optimism to Existentialism. 1969, 1947

A vision of song festival culture as rooted in the symbiosis of song, soil, and nation was also deployed as a primary organizational motif in the documentary film *Leelo*, written by the Estonian poet Hando Runnel, directed by Jüri Müür, about the 1969 song festival. Yet the film's opening sequence carries clear existentialist tones.

The first scene opens with the camera moving slowly through the pine forest (Figures 27–28). Then a male voiceover recites a quasi-apocalyptic vision from a folk song:

> Sooner will leaf disappear from the tree,
> the leaf from the tree, the berry from the ground,
> sooner will the fish be gone from the sea,
> the water vanish from the spring,
> the water vanish from the river,
> before our songs will end.[145]

**Figures 27–28** Stills from the film Leelo, 1969, directed by Jüri Müür.

---

[145] Jüri Müür, *Leelo. Eesti laulupidude sajandijuubelilt. Juuni 1969* (Tallinnfilm, 1969).

The camera then tracks along a small dirt path through the forest, then glides through a sequence of empty village roads to reach a larger paved road – still totally empty – before it then arrives on the early morning streets of Tartu, the university town, where at last some human figures appear: solitary singers whom the camera tracks as they walk to reach the Tartu song festival grounds where the conductor Gustav Ernesaks signals the choir to commence its song. These scenes are accompanied by singing voices that finally burst into full force as the camera arrives at the male choir.

The special unorthodoxy of *Leelo*'s beginning becomes especially visible in comparison with an earlier song festival documentary, the 1947 film *Laulev rahvas* [*The Singing Nation*]. The imaginary of song, soil, and nation, expressed in 1969, was likewise present in earlier decades of Soviet rule: as with *Leelo*, the 1947 *Laulev rahvas* also opens with the assemblage of land and song. Even as the whole film is strongly colored by the rhetoric of Stalinist state building, the opening scenes present images of nature, with human-made objects nowhere visible, and a female choir faintly audible on the soundtrack. The first words of the voiceover, pronounced in the characteristically bright Stalinist mode, declare that "All across midsummer Estonia, there sounds a song. Meadowlands and pastures re-echo it, the forest lake listens in thoughtfully."[146] Young women in picturesque folk costumes are then seen picking their way through the landscape, up a small hill, together with workers carrying traditional hay rakes, the group disappearing and reappearing in the tall grass and at last joining a singing choir on the hilltop (Figures 29–31).

The film goes on to track singers and musicians streaming into Tallinn from all over the country: an overcrowded sailboat arriving with singers from an island (Figure 32), miners from Kohtla-Järve climbing into an open truck, and so forth. In this, the film repeats, albeit with the requisite Stalinist optimism, the pre-Soviet pattern of "narrating the song festival." And it was, indeed, a remarkable achievement that small singing collectives from different regions of the country would find their way to Tartu, in 1869, for a communal *priiusepidu* [*freedom festival*], as the main organizer Johann Voldemar Jannsen unofficially called the first song festival.[147]

In the 1969 film *Leelo*, the camera again follows singers heading to Tallinn, now carrying the symbolic festival flame; it includes also a sequence of men with torches, wearing simple traditional linen clothing, leaving an ancient castle site on horseback. The following sequence displays the imagery of the seashore,

---

[146] Nikolai Komarevtsev, *Laulev rahvas* (Tallinna Kinokroonika Stuudio, Leningradi Dokumentaalfilmide Kinostuudio, 1947).
[147] Põldmäe, *Esimene Eesti üldlaulupidu 1869*, 33–38.

**Figures 29–31** Stills from the film Laulev rahvas [The Singing Nation, 1947], directed by Nikolay Komavertsev.

**Figures 29–31** (cont.).

**Figure 32** Still from the film Laulev rahvas.

the sea, whereupon the camera then reaches the festival grounds, and continues with long shots of a traditional farm dwelling – all while the choir sings the cantata *Laulu algus* [*The Birth of a Song*, music by Veljo Tormis, words by Hando Runnel]: "A century away, on the shores of Estonia, a song began ... This song started in a humble house."[148] This cantata was among the first songs presented on the 1969 song festival program: *Koit*, the opening song (discussed earlier) was followed by *Lenini partei* [*Lenin's Party*], followed by *Laulu algus*. *Lenin's party* was the only song of the first festival concert to carry the explicit party-political message.

Notwithstanding their common use of nature imagery, the differences between the 1969 and the 1947 song festival films are nevertheless striking. The connection between song and nature grounds the narrative in both films, as we have observed, but in the 1947 documentary, the landscape is soon populated by a joyous gathering of singers, whereas the 1969 documentary persists much longer in a filmic meditation that follows along a series of empty roads. Both films had to be approved by the censors, of course. The opening of the 1969 film might be justified by the early morning hours and by the artistic aspiration to present a poetic trajectory from initial quietude to full jubilation in later parts of the film. Even so, the dark, existential undertones of its opening scenes are striking, especially in combination with the voiceover that recites a folk verse about the persistence of song, whatever catastrophes might later befall the human and natural worlds. These gloomy notes were in tune with themes of environmental devastation and vulnerability – Rachel Carson's book *Silent Spring* had been published in Estonian translation in 1968 – but also with the new restrictions of the Soviet regime, and more generally with the "existentialist" cultural moods that had spread all over Europe.

### The Late 1980s Decolonization: Song Power Joins the Environmental Protest Movement

In 1988, the song festival tradition achieved its fullest decolonizing potential in a set of protest actions now known as the "Singing Revolution." The choral tradition had been repurposed into a set of peaceful demonstrations that combined speeches and song. The Estonian blue, black, and white tricolor, the display of which was strictly forbidden during the Soviet decades, was first openly unfurled once more during the Tartu Music Days, in May 1988, during a performance of the "Five Fatherland Songs" cycle. These five songs by Alo

---

[148] Müür, *Leelo*.

Mattiisen (for the musical arrangement) and Jüri Leesment (for the lyrics of four songs) were creative reworkings of nineteenth-century patriotic verses, set to rock accompaniment; they quickly became emblematic tunes of the burgeoning protest movement against Soviet rule. On July 1, 1988, the tricolors of all three pre-Soviet Baltic republics were openly displayed in Vilnius, Lithuania, during Gaudeamus, the song festival of Baltic university students.[149] When, later in July, the Latvian national flag publicly flew in Riga for the first time in Soviet-era Latvia, it was once again in the context of a festival for song and dance – this time during the Baltica folklore festival.[150]

The late 1980s decolonizing movement once again made free use of nature imagery and associations, yet nineteenth-century songs now accrued another layer of anticolonial critique: they were repurposed, with new rhythms and new melodies and new lyrical interpolations referring to the present-day political situation.[151] Original lyrical themes were recast in the direction of more open critique: where nineteenth-century festival repertoires had been carefully screened by imperial censors, by 1988, censorship in glasnost-era Estonia had lost its battle against the new era.

The changing times gave a new, often more pointed context for critique: the romantic glorification of a beautiful homeland was now supplemented with accusations of environmental devastation, excessive migration, and the presence of a foreign army. In *Kaunimad laulud* [*The most beautiful songs*], a song with original lyrics by Peeter Ruubel, the poet declares its devotion to his homeland: "I dedicate to you, dear homeland / the most beautiful of songs." The new version dialogically inverts the initial pathos and redirects it toward naked social critique:

> The most beautiful of songs
> were left unsung
> in an endless array of slogans, flags, and promises.
> The most beautiful of wishes
> remained unfulfilled
> in an array of contentment, rubles, and foolishness.

In another song from the same cycle, *Minge üles mägedelle* [*Go high atop the hills*], with original lyrics by Karl August Hermann, rewritten by Henno Käo, the original lyric calls upon its listeners to "go high atop the hills" and then

---

[149] By this time, the pre-Soviet Lithuanian flag had already been displayed openly, in the context of a different meeting.
[150] Arnolds Klotiņš, "The Latvian Neo-Folklore Movement and the Political Changes of the Late 20th Century," *The World of Music* 44, no. 3 (2002): 123.
[151] Annus, *Soviet Postcolonial Studies: A View from the Western Borderlands*, 166–67.

evokes naturecultural imagery: the vista of one's beautiful homeland, with its forests and flowers, lakes and rivers, pasturelands and fields of grain. In the new version by Henno Käo, the same call is followed by a dismal catalogue of new realities: the hilltop panorama is tainted by the presence of a "silent, foreign army" and obstructed by the new Soviet-era high-rise district of Lasnamäe, which was then inhabited almost exclusively by new Russophone settlers and, as the new lyric would have it, was "a boil upon the limestone clint." The sense is plainly one of human conflict, but it gains its power through its figuration as something more: the land itself has come to suffer septicity and contamination.

The historical continuities are striking – in 1988, the ritual of collective singing, by kindling collective affect and binding it to nature imagery, gave voice once again to dissent and helped fortify decolonization. But this time, by capitalizing on the opportunity opened up by Gorbachev-era reforms and later also by growing political turmoil in Russia, decolonization processes in the Baltics could develop to their full potential and culminate with Estonia, Latvia, and Lithuania regaining their political statehood.

In this, choral song culture intertwined with the environmental protest movement: opposition to major new phosphorite mines, which had been waged by scientists and officials since 1972, developed into a mass movement known as the "Phosphorite War" in 1987.[152] The northeast Estonian phosphorite and oil shale mines, which were directly under the jurisdiction of the central authorities in Moscow, fouled the landscape, polluted the environment, and occasioned the importing of new settlers to supply industrial plants with new labor, all without any visible benefit for the locals. Such a clear case of colonial eco-social violence was ideal material to arouse mass protest – and, indeed, environmental causes were a major trigger for mass protests across the Soviet Union, in Latvia, Moldova, Kazakhstan, and elsewhere.

The critique of colonial-style carelessness and ruinous extractivism was evocatively presented in a cartoon by Priit Pärn in May 1987, in the weekly *Sirp ja Vasar*: a sturdy peasant in a dilapidated cart, drawn by a horse on the verge of collapse, spreads manure on a vast, desolate field (Figure 33). A pitchfork-full of manure, thrown from the cart, is shaped like a silhouette of Estonia, with the peculiar contour of the two biggest islands making it impossible for locals to miss the connection. The text of the cartoon is brief and to the point: "Just shit ... " – an expression commonly used in vulgar Estonian for stuff that fails and one can't be bothered with. The message of the cartoon is twofold:

---

[152] Mihkel Veiderma, "Fosforiidiuurimine Eestis – Kas pidu või ohust ajendatud tegevus?," *Akadeemia*, no. 3 (2000): 626–33; Juhan Aare, *Fosforiidisõda 1971–1989* (Tallinn: Kirilille Kirjastus, 1999).

**Figure 33** Priit Pärn, Just Shit! 1987. Ink on paper. Author's private collection.

most obviously, the Russian peasant carelessly disposes of Estonia's interests; Estonia is something that can be easily discarded as "mere shit." At the same time, the caricature references plans for phosphorite mining: Estonia and its interests are cast aside in order to provide fertilizer for the USSR, even as the vastness of Russia itself means that damaging extractions from tiny Estonia could hardly provide any meaningful difference. Yet the Russian, his cart hitched to a downtrodden horse on the verge of collapse, doesn't care in the least; his actions are without thought; he has his back to the damage in his wake – what he calls shit and what Estonians call their homeland. The scrub on the line of horizon is presumably vegetation, but was interpreted by some as the towers of the Kremlin in Moscow. The cartoon became widely popular and was reproduced on posters and on protest t-shirts.[153]

## Conclusion: Not Merely Ecological Nationalism

We've seen how anticolonial struggles bridge times and traditions in their recourse to figure of nature. Anticolonial exigencies sustained the nineteenth-century Romantic tradition of choral song festivals, down through the modern

---

[153] Mari Laaniste, "Pilt ja hetk: 'Sitta kah!' juhtum," in *Pilt tänapäeva kultuuris. Võitlusvälja laienemine. Etüüde nüüdiskultuurist*; 9, ed. Virve Sarapik, Mari Laaniste, and Neeme Lopp (Tallinn: Eesti Kunstiakadeemia Kirjastus, 2021), 148–159.

era of existentialism and space travel, and up into the postmodern era. In this context, nature imagery lent its energies to the anticolonial cause, helping to sustain a sense of national belonging and, in the late 1980s, offering a format for nonviolent dissent that combined environmental concerns with calls for sovereignty.

At the same time, the environmental sensibility that gave affective power to songs of protest went beyond mere "ecological nationalism," a combination of land and nation for the purposes of a politics of liberation. The choral song repertoire and its accompanying cultural fantasies included more than just a celebration of nationhood through nature-imagery; the songs also manifested personal or communal belonging together with natural environments. While national sensibilities are clearly expressed in the song festival repertoire, this is not a relationship of surrogacy as in Jane Dawson's interpretation of eco-nationalism, where nationalists are presumed to "mask their intentions behind a surrogate cause."[154] Rather, the nature imagery and sense of national belonging form a complementary relationship, in which national identity is given particularity and made intimate through familiar references to the beauty of homely landscapes.

But if the song-land-nation complex formed an important strand, it was not the dominant strand, among Estonian imaginaries of nature in the twentieth century. The Schweitzer-influenced local-global imaginary, discussed in Section 1, was able to tie a personally felt ethical responsibility with planetary concerns. The experience of the forbidden sea (Section 2), similarly, reverberated through people's intimate personal connections with natural surroundings. In the next section, we will introduce further ambiguity to era-specific imaginaries of nature.

The song-land-nation complex, discussed in this section, bound people together with a sense for their common national belonging and then directed this sense into a powerful decolonizing force. It supported and shaped a mass-level affective response, yet it also produced some cultural dissonance. The birth of song from the waves and the wind, the beauty of verdant gardens, the fecundity of one's own dead body joined to the fatherland – these metaphysically charged visions were out of sync of the late industrial era. What about irony and laughter? What about doubt and ambiguity? Cynicism and cybernetics? Because such romantic earnestness was historically out of phase with everyday moods of the era, it had to be revived and cultivated on festival grounds and reproduced in accompanying publications before it could be put to use in the mass-protests of the late 1980s.

---

[154] Dawson, *Eco-Nationalism*, 163.

Anticolonial movements very typically include crude elements of essentialism – indeed the lack of a clearly defined enemy would be a hindrance and a challenge for any political struggle, especially one to regain national sovereignty. Simplifications and all-too-clear figurations of national boundaries and national belongings are part of this story. Nationally attuned images of nature, expressed and engaged through singing, were no exception – they, too, occasionally included crude us-them juxtapositions.[155] We might say, then, that the ghost of national essentialism hovers over this topic.

*I myself didn't sing in the song festival as a child – competition was heavy and our school choir didn't make the cut. For a majority of Estonians in the late Soviet era, the festival was rather a media event, to be followed on TV or on the radio. I was there on the festival grounds a few years ago though, in 2019, when my children were singing. The song festival tradition continues in Estonia, Latvia, and Lithuania, urged partly by the continuing threat from Russia that keeps alive the memory of past struggles against colonial rule, but also partly by the inertia and the pleasure of tradition.*

## 4 Urbanitis and Limits to Growth. 1978

### 1978: The Cybernetic Woman

On the cover of Aimée Beekman's novel *Valikuvõimalus* [*The Possibility of Choice*, 1978] stands the figure of a naked woman with a calculator in place of her womb (Figure 34). This novel, among the boldest and most controversial of Estonian Soviet-era writings, caused a stir in Estonian society of the late 1970s – or, more precisely, its main character Regina polarized and provoked both readers and critics.

Regina, an attractive, unmarried schoolteacher approaching her thirtieth birthday, leaves her fashionable life in the capital city of Tallinn after a sobering breakup with her lover. She relocates to a small provincial town, where she moves into a spacious house left to her by her aunt and made even more comfortable, psychologically at least, with her inheritance of the aunt's savings. Disillusioned with love and romantic notions of marital harmony, but determined to avoid the socially beset status assigned to single women, she herself proposes marriage to a mild-mannered local drunk. She then conceives three children from carefully timed one-night stands, each with a different partner, all with clean medical records – alcoholism, as Regina was well aware, would potentially cause birth defects and brain damage in children.[156] By the end, she

---

[155] For more concerning essentialist elements of popular patriotic songs in late 1980s, see Annus, *Soviet Postcolonial Studies: A View from the Western Borderlands*, 166–67, 172.

[156] Compare to Hugo Remmelg, "'Eluvesi' ja meie järglased," *Horisont*, no. 9 (1980): 13–16.

**Figure 34** Aimée Beekman's novel Valikuvõimalus [The Possibility of Choice]. Tallinn: Eesti Raamat, 1978. By Jaan Tammsaar.

comes to make plans to conceive a fourth child with her husband, who has developed over the years into an exemplary father. As the novel follows Regina's "calculated" actions, it provides a running critical commentary on a modern society in crisis.

Regina is presented as a product of the cybernetic era, someone whose life is almost grotesquely regulated by rational decisions. Repeatedly, Regina sees her decision-making protocols as a kind of programming analogous to those used in computers:

> With her aunt's savings book in hand, a new thought had automatically presented itself to Regina: now I can feed into myself any program, she thought. The initial data were promising: a spacious house to live in; a garden

for direct contact with nature (digging in the soil had become fashionable among people weary of artificial environments); a job at a good school – what more could she want?[157]

Indeed Regina's as-if-cybernetic body seems to function faultlessly. With remarkable ease, it produces one child after another from her one-night stands, until, with the third child, her planned pregnancy scenario goes awry: in the morning after conception, Regina awakens to find herself in bed with another man, and not her intended partner. This other man turns out to have a suboptimal clinical record – thus compromising Regina's program for conceiving healthy children.

The novel is remarkable for its proliferative ambiguity. Regina's character is presented as admirable in her determination and agency, but also as a symptom of a society in crisis, indeed a "slag from the overheated cauldron of civilization."[158] The novel views its era through a set of symptomatic crises: extramarital relations and broken relationships had become the norm, as people – "poisoned with noise" and addicted to constant stimulation – moved along on the "conveyer belt" of easy pleasures.[159] In this "era of superficiality," people in the cities were figured as suffering from *urbanitis*, a malady of urban life that made people impatient and fidgety and inclined to fill their days with meaningless quotidian trivialities.[160] Regina also observes that the widespread pollution of water and air had, in effect, created a permanent experiment, testing how much degradation human health could tolerate.[161] In the novel's view, there, at the outset of the information age, humanity was suffering a deep and multifaceted global crisis: growing commodification, unrestrained urbanization, and polluted air and water were all producing a sense of shared insecurity and uncertainty, impacting the most intimate spheres of everyday life.

Beekman's novel certainly hit a nerve.[162] For some, the novel was too old-fashioned in its criticism: the eminent critic and poet Ene Mihkelson (b. 1944), ten years younger than Beekman (b. 1933) (Figure 35), bluntly declared the novel a failure for its uncritical acquiescence to outdated patriarchal social norms and for focusing on social status rather than valuing each person's unique contribution regardless of marital status.[163] And, as if to indicate that Regina's calculative programs were outdated, the same October 13th issue of the weekly *Sirp ja Vasar* that published Mihkelson's review also published the translation of a short story, "Announcement," by the Mexican writer Juan José Arreola,

---

[157] Aimée Beekman, *Valikuvõimalus* (Tallinn: Eesti Raamat, 1978), 56.   [158] Beekman, 152.
[159] Beekman, 10, 38.   [160] Beekman, 38, 132.   [161] Beekman, 99.
[162] Johanna Ross, "Aimée Beekmani 'Valikuvõimalus': Ühe omanäolise romaani vastuvõtu dünaamikast," *Methis. Studia Humaniora Estonica* 6, no. 8 (2011): 21–35.
[163] Ene Mihkelson, "Valikuvõimalus valikuvabaduseta," *Sirp ja Vasar*, October 13, 1978.

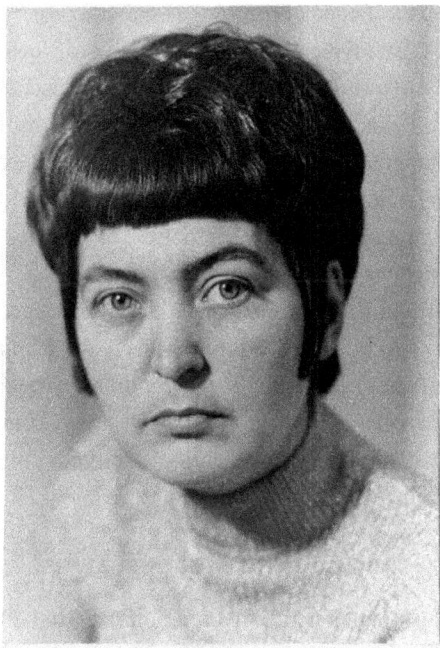

**Figure 35** Aimee Beekman, 1975. Estonian Literary Museum, EKLA B-142-6. Unknown photographer.

featuring Plastisex, an artificial woman who executes commands transmitted from a control panel.[164]

Among those who reacted to Beekman's novel was Gustav Naan, once a devoted Stalinist but now a liberal scientist and a popular public speaker. Naan, born in Vladivostok, was among those who were sent to Estonia to establish Soviet rule after the annexation – yet he successfully switched gears in the post-Stalin years and, for a time, attained a degree of local prestige. In 1960, as the vice-president of the Estonian Academy of Sciences, Naan managed to secure permission from Moscow to open the Institute of Cybernetics in Tallinn.[165] With his background in physics, he played an active role in the 1960s–1970s cybernetics boom; he also wrote an introduction to the 1969 Estonian translation of a book

---

[164] Juan José Arreola, "Teade," transl by Jüri Talvet. *Sirp ja Vasar*, November 13, 1978.

[165] "Kolme mehe kõnelused [Nikolai Alumäe, Boris Tamm, Hillar Aben]. Kirja pannud Rein Veskimäe," *Horisont*, no. 9 (1980); Virve Sarapik, "Küberneetika ja semiootika: Tõrksa taltsutamine ehk kokkupuuteid 1960. aastate nõukogude abstraktse kunstiga," *Kunstiteaduslikke Uurimusi* 29, no. 1–2 (2020): 35–62. Regrettably, in his history of Soviet cybernetics, Slava Gerovitch does not even refer to the existence of the Institutes of Cybernetics in Tallinn and in Tbilisi, both founded in 1960. Slava Gerovitch, *From Newspeak to Cyberspeak: A History of Soviet Cybernetics* (Cambridge, MA: MIT Press, 2004).

by Norbert Wiener, the famous originator of cybernetics.[166] In Naan's popular writings of the 1970s, he typically addressed themes of love, sex, and marriage from the perspective of a cool-minded scientist; he also discussed global concerns of population growth and food shortages.[167] In many writings, he supported prejudice-free sexual practices, including openness toward extramarital relationships, and he fiercely attacked what he considered outdated Christian norms of fidelity.[168] Indeed arguably, Naan's promotion of sexual liberation was one impetus behind the conception of Beekman's novel.

When Beekman's novel was published, Naan announced his approval of Regina's choices – yet, like the critic Ene Mihkelson, he expressed his disappointment with the novel's apparent disdain for unmarried women.[169] In related conversations in the Russian media, in *Literaturnaya Gazeta*, Naan adopted a more reserved tone, promoting a scientific, analytical approach over mere moralizing complaints.[170]

## Do You Suffer from Urbanitis?

The reception of Beekman's novel was too polarized to be lauded simply as a great success, but its sense of a society in crisis certainly reflected the mood of its era. Similar sentiments had been often expressed in both media and fiction – urbanitis, for example, a term used in the novel, had circulated in the media for over a decade before its publication.[171]

Harri Jänes expounded upon the symptoms of urbanitis at length in his article *Urbaniit [Urbanitis]*, which earned him the annual prize of the *Sirp ja Vasar* cultural weekly in 1966.[172] According to Jänes, the term first appeared in a publication of the World Health Organization in 1964; this phenomenon, as he explained, presents itself through "diseases and disorders of the nervous system,

---

[166] Gustav Naan, "Norbert Wiener ja ajastu mõttelaad," in *Inimolendite inimlik kasutamine. Küberneetika ja ühiskond.* Translated by Boris Kabur. LR 1969, Nr 45–47, 1969, 5–11. Wiener's book *Cybernetics: Or Control and Communication in the Animal and the Machine* had already been translated into Estonian in 1961; both books came out in Russian in 1958.

[167] Gustav Naan, "Kas tagasi matriarhaati?," *Looming*, no. 4, 5 (1976): 634–653; 801–823.

[168] Naan. See also Gustav Naan, "Su(u)ndmõtteid armastusabielust," *Sirp ja Vasar*, 14.05; 21.05; 28. 05; 4.06; 11.06; 18.06; 25.06, 1976; Eve Annuk, "Soodiskursustest Eesti nõukogude perioodil," *Ariadne Lõng*, no. 1/2 (2015): 70–89.

[169] Gustav Naan, "Irviku Kiisu naeratuse lummuses," *Horisont*, no. 3 (1980): 18–21.

[170] Gustav Naan, "On, ona i vtoroy zakon termodynamiki," *Literaturnaya Gazeta*, September 15, 1976. Vladimir Shlapentokh lauded this article as "one of the most brilliant attempts to apply refined scholarly concepts to marriage." Vladimir Shlapentokh, *Love, Marriage, and Friendship in the Soviet Union: Ideals and Practices* (New York: Praeger, 1984), 95.

[171] Endel Mallene, "Missuguse informatsiooni tulvast on jutt?," *Looming*, no. 4 (1976): 689–90; Harald Keres, "Suurest meiest väikeste eelkäijate taustal. Järelemõtlemisi teemal teadus, aeg, inimkond," *Horisont*, no. 2 (1972): 3–8; Mats Traat, *Rippsild* (Tallinn: Eesti Raamat, 1979), 107.

[172] Harri Jänes, "Urbaniit," *Sirp ja Vasar*, April 8, 1966.

**Figure 36** According to Harri Jänes, architectural monotony contributed to urbanitis. Residential housing in Mustamäe, 1969–1970. National Archives of Estonia, EFA.242.0.93712. Unknown photographer.

heart, circulatory system, digestive organs, and metabolism."[173] Rushing, transportation stress, noise pollution, everyday irritations, architectural monotony, highly refined foods, polluted air – all this contributed to urbanitis (see Figure 36). Jänes laid out the dire – indeed the fatal – consequences of urbanitis: chronic constipation leading to weight gain and premature death. Yet a good half of the article is dedicated to the topic of air and water pollution. "If this were to continue," warns Jänes, "then soon the air of our planet will no longer be fit for breathing."[174] Jänes emphasizes in particular the need to spend plenty of time in the fresh air: "One must, every day, spend at least 1.5 hours outdoors; on weekends, it should be 3–4 hours."[175]

In the media, concerns for the stress and pollution of urban life were commonly articulated by way of global comparisons.[176] Typically, essayists saw little reason to regard the Soviet Union as in any way superior to the West. Harri Jänes, for example, brings out Perm and Moscow as negative examples: in Perm, reportedly, only seventeen trees or bushes had been planted over the

---

[173] Jänes, 6.   [174] Jänes, 7.   [175] Jänes, 7.
[176] Heino Tonsiver, "Linnastumine ühiskondliku tööjaotuse aspektist," in *Majandusteadus ja rahvamajandus. Aastaraamat 1969/70* (Tallinn: Eesti Raamat, 1971), 144–56; Silvia Vissak, "Kas pestitsiidid või biotõrje?," *Edasi*, July 7, 1966; "Tark inimene ja loodus. NLKP XXIV kongressi järgseid mõtteid," *Eesti Loodus*, no. 6 (1971): 321–23.

course of forty-seven years, and in Moscow's environs, meadows and forest flowers had more or less disappeared.[177] Scientists drew upon data variously from capitalist cities, from the USSR, and from Estonia itself: Heino Tonsiver's article about urbanization established its statistical context with data from Tokyo, London, and New York, and he referred to similarities between urbanization tendencies in New York and Moscow. Harri Jänes presented data about pollution levels in the United States – and then saluted a 1960 California law, which required new cars sold in the state to be equipped with a PCV valve for the complete combustion of exhaust gases.[178] The fiction-minded Jaan Eilart quoted Antoine de Saint-Exupéry, John Steinbeck, Rachel Carson, as well as the Estonian poets Debora Vaarandi and Ly Seppel, and he ended his essay about the human devastation of nature with a quote from Friedrich Engels – as if all these writers stood united in support of one shared conviction.[179] In the context of this concern, there could be no iron curtain: the world was one common space grappling with a similar set of problems everywhere.

## Anthropocene Art of the 1960s–1970s

While Aimée Beekman was writing her novel, her husband Vladimir Beekman, the chairman of the Estonian Writers' Union and a chemist by education, was working on his own novel *Eesli aasta* [*The Year of the Donkey*, 1979], published a year later. *Eesli aasta* is a gloomy dystopia about the destruction of an indigenous island community after the discovery of precious phosphates on their land. The novel's nonlocal extractors make their argument: "The world faces overpopulation, every loaf of bread and every bag of fertilizer is increasingly precious, because we and our children might soon face starvation. We cannot leave such a reserve in the ground!"[180] As Beekman later explained in his memoirs, the novel was inspired by plans of the central government to start excavating phosphorite in Toolse, on the north coast of Estonia – a project that Estonian scientists and local politicians managed to obstruct and delay for more than a decade, until its forceful reactivation triggered mass protests in 1987–88.[181]

Aimée and Vladimir Beekman were hardly the only writers concerned about pollution, careless colonial-style extraction of natural resources, and other troubling tendencies of the era. An earlier section of this Element discussed the impact of the 1962 publication of Rachel Carson's *Silent Spring* (fully translated into Estonian in 1968). Estonian literary scholars point to Carson's

---

[177] Jänes, "Urbaniit." [178] Jänes.
[179] Jaan Eilart, "Kotkapoegadest, veest, mullast ja muust," *Noorte Hääl*, April 17, 1965.
[180] Vladimir Beekman, *Eesli aasta* (Tallinn: Eesti Raamat, 1979), 14.
[181] Elle-Mari Talivee, "Juhtumiuuring: Vladimir Beekman, Nõukogude Liidu energia- ja sõjatööstus ning fosforiidisõda," *Methis* 30 (2022): 69–81.

work as a watershed for Estonian environmental fiction, and they note an intensification of environmental awareness over the course of the 1970s – although, one must add that, in poetry, these themes had been in evidence since the second half of the 1960s.[182] Novelists and poets drew attention to pesticides causing death of bee-populations and animals – even sending a very human toddler into hospital care (Osvald Tooming, Mats Traat); they addressed the devastation of oil spills (Aino Pervik), river pollution (Kersti Merilaas), and more.

The visual arts also contributed powerfully to these explorations. Ilmar Malin's painting *Kustuv päike* [*Fading Sun*] from 1968 is considered "the inaugural event of Anthropocene art" in Estonian art history:[183] in the painting, the blackened sun recalls the shape of a nuclear mushroom cloud, and the Earth below it appears as a barren geological surface (Figure 37). Many other works

**Figure 37** Ilmar Malin, Fading Sun. 1968. Synthetic tempera and mixed media on fibreboard. Art Museum of Estonia.

---

[182] Timo Maran and Kadri Tüür, eds., *Eesti looduskultuur* (Tartu: Eesti Kirjandusmuuseum, 2005), 263.
[183] Linda Kaljundi, "Sissejuhatuseks. Milleks veel üks antropotseeninäitus ja mis võiks olla sellest kasu eesti kunstiajaloole?," in *Kunst antropotseeni ajastul = Art in the Age of the Anthropocene*, ed. Linda Kaljundi and Karin Vicente (Tallinn: Eesti Kunstimuuseum, 2023), 19.

of art in this period – by Jüri Arrak, Kristiina Kaasik, Silvi Liiva, Jüri Palm, Tiit Pääsuke, Ludmilla Siim, Olev Soans, Rein Tammik, Olga Terri, Andres Tolts, Vello Vinn, and others – drew attention to pollution and to other forms of environmental devastation.

## The Limits to Growth

It was also about this time, in the 1970s, that global concern became more pronounced with respect to the destructive long-term consequences of the exploitation of limited natural resources. In 1968, an international think tank seeking to address pressing global problems was founded under the name of the Club of Rome; its first report, *The Limits to Growth*, was published in 1972, presenting the results of computer modeling to predict possible global scenarios for the future. For Estonian readers, the main conclusion of *The Limits to Growth* was comprehensively summarized by Jaak Allik in the journal *Looming* in 1976: "If current trends in population growth, industrialisation, pollution, food production and resource depletion continue unabated, limits will be reached within the next 100 years."[184] A similar verdict had already reached Estonian readers in 1974 in the newspaper *Edasi*, when Vello Pohla, recently returned from Moscow's Lomonosov Institute for Raising the Qualification of Lecturers in Social Sciences, admitted that lectures on the ecological crisis were "rather shocking."[185] Pohla reproduced the official Moscow parlance and called *The Limits to Growth* a devastating verdict on capitalism: "It argues that, unless, within the next 10 years, there can be instituted radical changes in human thinking, social life, production, etc., then any possible framework of functionality for human life on earth will be headed for collapse by 2100."[186] A week after Pohla's article, the overview of a 1974 United Nations conference made its way from the American weekly *Newsweek*, to the Russian weekly *Za Rubezhom*, to the Estonian daily *Edasi*: there, *The Limits to Growth* report was discussed in the context of demographic explosions and food shortages in African, Asian, and Latin American countries.[187]

---

[184] Jaak Allik, "Ökoloogiline kriis? Prognoosid ja tegelikkus," *Looming*, no. 1 (1976): 126.

[185] Vello Pohla, "Moskva-märkmeid," *Sirp ja Vasar*, September 20, 1974. Concerning *The Limits to Growth* in Russian media and scientific publications, see Donald R. Kelley, "Economic Growth and Environmental Quality in the USSR: Soviet Reaction to 'The Limits to Growth,'" *Canadian Slavonic Papers* 18, no. 3 (1976): 266–83; Julia Lajus, "Soviet Official Critiques of the Resource Scarcity Prediction by Limits to Growth Report: The Case of Evgenii Fedorov's Ecological Crisis Rhetoric," *European Review of History: Revue Européenne d'histoire* 27, no. 3 (2020): 321–41.

[186] Pohla, "Moskva-märkmeid"; Mart Port, "Linnaehituse tulevikuprobleeme," *Ehitus ja Arhitektuur*, no. 2 (1975): 3–7; Tõnis Värnik, "Liiga palju inimesi? 'Newsweek', New York," *Edasi*, September 26, 1974.

[187] Värnik, "Liiga palju inimesi?"

A thorough explanation, with charts and columns of data from *The Limits to Growth*'s projection of the global future, together with the implications of all this for city planning, was published by the architect Mart Port in the journal *Ehitus ja Arhitektuur* [*Building and Architecture*, 1975]. Later years of the 1970s saw a great diffusion of interest in *The Limits to Growth* report and in other computerized models for future scenarios, neither of which chined of optimism.

When Aimée Beekman's novel was first published in 1978 in issues 1–3 of the journal *Looming*, the first issue also included a lengthy article by Toomas Sutt *Evolutsioon – inimesega või inimeseta* [*Evolution – with or without Human Beings*]. Sutt observed coolly that "the consequences of human activity threaten to eliminate the necessary biological prerequisites for the existence of humanity."[188] Sutt also had one dubious consolation to offer: "In the event that humanity should fail to avoid an ecological catastrophe, this does not, of course, mean the cessation of biological evolution – simply that evolution will continue without Homo sapiens."[189]

In early January 1979, Tallinn itself hosted an important international symposium on "Trends and Perspectives in the Development of Science and Technology and Their Impact on Solutions to Contemporary Global Problems," in preparation for the UN Conference on Science and Technology for Development to be held later, in August 1979, in Vienna. The Tallinn symposium, organized jointly by the UN Advisory Committee on the Application of Science and Technology to Development and by the USSR State Committee on Science and Technology, included an impressive set of participants. In Walter Clemens' account, "Of the more than fifty foreigners invited, many were associated either with IIASA or the Club of Rome; others included officials from the UN Environmental Program, UNESCO, and other UN agencies."[190] Coverage of this event in the Estonian media was free of any criticism toward Club of Rome reports and other computer-generated models outlining possible future scenarios. Global problems were deemed to be of primary importance; the fact that they impacted the whole of humanity called for a joint response from all over the world. This seriousness was in stark contrast with the rejective optimism that had accompanied some earlier commentaries.[191] Now it was declared that "The

---

[188] Toomas Sutt, "Evolutsioon- inimesega või inimeseta," *Looming*, no. 1 (1978): 88.
[189] Sutt, 88–89.
[190] Walter C. Clemens, *Can Russia Change? The USSR Confronts Global Interdependence* (London: Routledge, 2012), 147. IIASA stands for "International Institute for Applied Systems Analysis." About its activities, see Egle Rindzeviciute, *The Power of Systems: How Policy Sciences Opened up the Cold War World* (Ithaca: Cornell University Press, 2016).
[191] "Globaalprobleemid. Tallinna sümpoosion," *Sirp ja Vasar*, January 19, 1979.

scientists, including Club of Rome members, politicians, and administrators who attended the meeting were united in their understanding that humanity was, in some sense, approaching a limit in its evolution, a limit that demanded change from its old ways ..."[192]

In 1981, the writer Mati Unt, celebrated for his special talent for sensing and documenting the tendencies of his era, had marked a change in public attitudes. Unt surveyed ten titles issued by the Club of Rome between 1971 and 1980: "In the early seventies, the Club of Rome was regarded as a scaremonger, but now they try to outdo it in an ever-escalating pessimism. And indeed, it is hard to be an optimist when you hear, for example, that tropical rainforests are being destroyed at the rate of 50 hectares per minute."[193] Unt quotes Aurelio Peccei, the president of the Club of Rome: "The eighties will be the decisive decade. [...] We need to rectify the present situation in which rich white men are making all the decisions."[194]

Unt, in his characteristic mode – detached, observant, somewhat amused – assembles a catalogue of global problems dominating the discourse of the era:

> uncontrollable population growth, ethnic conflicts, social injustice, hunger and malnutrition, poverty and unemployment, obsession with growth, inflation, energy crisis, democracy crisis, currency crisis, protectionism, illiteracy, outdated education, youth rebellion, alienation, urban growth and decline, crime, rural depopulation, drugs, air pollution, violence, disregard for human rights, abuse of laws, atomic obsession, political corruption, bureaucracy, militarism, decline in faith and morality, general uncertainty.[195]

Aimée Beekman's character Regina would have eagerly endorsed Unt's list. Notably, however, in 1981, Unt's long list of global issues does not yet include climate change, even as the rising levels of $CO_2$ in the atmosphere and its potential for causing global warming were already noted in the 1972 *Limits to Growth* report and had been mentioned in Estonian-language commentaries.

By 1981, a thoroughly detailed analysis of computer-generated future scenarios had reached Estonian readers: Lembit Valt and Edgar Savisaar, both connected with Moscow research institutes, published first a series of articles and then a 1983 book *Globaalprobleemid ja tulevikustsenaariumid* [*Global Problems and Future Scenarios*]. Some of this work derived from Savisaar's dissertation, which he had written under Valt's supervision, on the socio-philosophical foundations of the global models of the Club of Rome, and defended in 1980 at Moscow State University. Savisaar became one of the leading figures in the early

---

[192] Jüri Roosaare and Ülo Mander, "Ökoloogiline kriis ja maailmamudelid," *Eesti Loodus*, no. 8 (1979): 522.
[193] Mati Unt, "Kas noored päästavad maailma?," *Looming*, no. 11 (1981): 1645.
[194] Unt, "Kas noored päästavad maailma?"  [195] Unt, 1645.

stages of Perestroika and later had a long, if sometimes controversial, political career with the restoration of independence.

Experience and expertise in future-planning and computer analysis, generated in the last Soviet decades in Estonian research centers, would later prove useful in working through the complex decisions facing Estonian economic and sociopolitical systems as they prepared to separate from the all-Union integrated model of economy and governance.[196] It took barely a decade to move from Aimée Beekman's 1978 "almost, but not quite" cybernetic vision of a society in crisis, to modeling a future self-governing Estonia in the late 1980s. Concerns for the global or planetary future lost some of their immediacy in the turbulent years of the late 1980s and 1990s, only to resurface once again, with renewed urgency, in the 21st century.

## Back to Nature? Failed Returns and Eco-ambiguity in the 1970s and Early 1980s

In discussions in the wake of *The Limits to Growth*, natural environments were figured as endangered, and urban environments as overcrowded and polluted. According to the 1979 census, 70 percent of Estonians were urban dwellers. Many of them, like Regina in Beekman's *Valikuvõimalus*, longed for greater contact with natural environments – indeed different ways of "encountering nature," whether in the form of weekend trips or some version of summer-homing, were part of the cultural script adopted by fashionable city-dwellers. Such aspirations made sense as a response to the multiple crises of the era: nature seemed to promise a healing counterbalance to civilizational distress.

In Beekman's *Valikuvõimalus*, Regina had regarded the large garden of her aunt's house as a special bonus of her inheritance. Her attitude changed once she settled in:

> Regina soon realized that gardening was beyond her strength and understanding. All around, smoke rose from chimneys, trees had their branches pruned, shrubs were trimmed, and the land was dug, raked, and sown with seeds. Regina's piece of land, by contrast, looked pitiful, with plants sprouting from the grass and yard waste, but Regina had no idea even of the names of these plants. In her own self-conception, she thought of herself as a nature lover; on a spring evening, she would walk for hours in the city parks, sharing with others her genuine enthusiasm for the buds and flowers bursting forth. Regina's hands-on interaction with the plant world had been quite modest, however, limited to budding cherry or chestnut branches in a vase. In

---

[196] Juhan Saharov, "Eesti perestroika keeled (1986–1988)," *Acta Historica Tallinnensia* 29, no. 1 (2023): 93–127.

retrospect, the love for nature often professed by city dwellers seemed embarrassingly meager.[197]

Regina hires a local hand to work her garden. She herself has a modest appreciation for nature – but she understands only its most domesticated appearances. In actuality, Regina – like many of her fellow city dwellers – has lost her connection to nature. Together with visions of deeply felt ecological attachments, discussed in previous sections, acknowledgment of one's lost contact with nature formed a common cultural current in the 1970s and early 1980s. For many, urban life, with all its crises and shortcomings, had simply become the new norm. In the well-known words of the Estonian poet Hando Runnel, from his 1978 collection:

> No longer does the soil offer much story for you,
> once you learn to walk on parquet floors,
> there, nature and the story of creation are forgotten
> and the sound of the fields fades from your ears.[198]

For Runnel, lost connection to fields and soil was a development to be mourned; many others took it coolly as a new fact of modern life. Both of these sentiments – longing for intimacy with nature and a sense of alienation from it – coexisted in culture, resulting in a diverse set of attachments and attitudes toward natural environments.

At the same time, the 1970s were an expansive era for nature-tourism: since 1968, a standard two-day weekend allowed people time for weekend getaways – especially since more and more families now were owners of personal cars.[199] Veljo Ranniku comments ironically on the emergence of a new species:

> Improved road conditions have made formerly remote woodlands and moorlands accessible, with decent gravel roads granting easy access to nature reserves. [...] We have come to see the emergence of a particular kind of a "motorised hiker": a one-hour-tourist, so to speak, who agrees to leave his vehicle, but for no more than one hour and at no greater distance than 500 metres.[200]

Ranniku exaggerates his point for ironic effect, yet the ambiguous figure of a motorized tourist was clearly part of the cultural landscape in this era. The one- or two-night camping trip, furnished with loud music and free-flowing alcohol, became an ironic fixture in stories and collections of the 1970s and early

---

[197] Beekman, *Valikuvõimalus*, 66.
[198] Hando Runnel, *Kodu-käija* (Tallinn: Eesti Raamat, 1978), 49. Runnel's verses (these and others) became well known through their musical adaptations by rock-groups like Ruja.
[199] Tõnu Jonuks and Atko Remmel, "Müüt eestlasest kui metsarahvast," *Keel ja Kirjandus*, no. 6 (2020): 459–82.
[200] Veljo Ranniku, "Turist kaitsealadel," *Eesti Loodus*, no. 5 (1976): 285.

1980s.[201] In fiction, one might find, side by side, both poetic celebrations of nature and satires upon the superficial quest for quick countryside rejuvenations.[202] The popular film *Siin me oleme! [Here We Are!*, 1978], written and directed by Sulev Nõmmik, was an especially successful satire of city people's efforts to "experience nature" over their summer vacation.

In Mati Unt's short story *Igavesti surev talu* [*The Farmstead Forever Dying*, 1973], the narrator walks around a derelict farm building and imagines himself filming its slowly creeping decay over the course of months and years. Unt desists from idealizing the decrepit farm: its last resident was a drunkard, and the rooms smell of decay. The narrator's interest in this place is purely aesthetic, yet, he declares, "I live in cities," and he distances himself even from his own imagined film project. He has no desire to spend any more time in this "backwater" place.[203]

## The Cranberry Crush

Perhaps the most environmentally ambiguous phenomenon of the 1960s and 1970s was the seasonal "cranberry crush": a surging mass of berry-pickers descending upon bogs and swamps during cranberry season. In 1965, strict regulations were put into place concerning times and methods of berry picking: one could start picking lingonberries on August 20, hazelnuts on September 1, and cranberries on September 15 (the dates thereafter would vary from year to year). Special cranberry harvesting tools were prohibited; breaking branches of hazelnut trees was strictly forbidden. It was announced beforehand that "Forest law and order is monitored primarily by state forest guards and auxiliary nature conservation inspectors."[204]

With these new regulations duly passed and published, people stormed the best-known cranberry swamps en masse on the very first day of the season. Edgar Kask contemplated the scene:

> The word cranberry has become the magnet that propels the motive force for wheels and minds in tens of thousands of cars and people every autumn. […] If it were possible to count the number of people who arrived at marshes on the first day of cranberry picking, the number would exceed the number of those who went to the Jubilee Song Festival. For years I have been following this cranberry crowd, unable to guess at the reasons behind its movement. Is it fashion or the body's hitherto unsuspected appetite for acidity? The desire to earn a few dozen rubles in a day, or the will to abandon the city and the four walls of home?[205]

---

[201] Aino Pervik, *Impulss* (Tallinn: Eesti Raamat, 1982).
[202] Jaan Kruusvall, *Armastuse esimene pool* (Tallinn: Eesti Raamat, 1973); Pervik, *Impulss*.
[203] Mati Unt, "Igavesti surev talu," in Mati Unt, Valitud teosed. 2 (Tallinn: Eesti Raamat, 1985), 185.
[204] Veljo Ranniku, "Millal minna seenele ja marjule," *Edasi*, August 17, 1965.
[205] Edgar Kask, *Tee vaikusesse. Muraka soostik* (Tallinn: Eesti Raamat, 1977), 56.

Kask himself arrives at the swamp before dawn, but he is far from being the first one there. By nine o'clock, the masses are there in force. Most will head back to their cars around four in the afternoon, and by the sunset, all is quiet again. Yet no one could say that the day had been spent in silent harmony with the berries and the few trees of the swamp lands; instead, Kask felt he had witnessed a great wave of "mass psychosis," a "noisy mass curiosity" and a "general hubbub."[206] But of course he is quite satisfied with his heavy load of berries when he leaves the swamp.

The cranberry crush ended with the 1970s. Seasonal regulations were lifted in 1981, as there was no longer any need to regulate the much-diminished berry picking. Partly too, the deepening of summer-home culture had given rise to a more plentiful substitute for mass-scale wild berry picking: strawberries, raspberries, and other homegrown berries could already fill cellars and storage spaces with jars of preserves. In new districts, full of prefabricated apartment buildings, people often lacked storage space for their homemade preserves anyway. By the early 1980s, wild berry picking had come to seem like a generational enthusiasm now in eclipse.[207] New generations had new passions and new practices.

*I'm wrapping up this topic in the late autumn of 2023. Harri Jänes's warnings of a premature death from urbanitis give me pause. An hour and a half in the fresh air on weekdays and 3–4 hours on the weekends: how can I possibly commit to such a discipline?*

*Yet urbanitis has come to seem like a joke, if we think back to the late 1970s understanding, shared across ideological divides, that global problems need global, joint responses, that the 1980s must bring change, and that rich white men should not have a monopoly on decisions about our global future. The COP28 (the 28th Conference of the Parties to the United Nations Framework Convention on Climate Change) has just ended with, once again, little more than nothing to address the continuing crisis of anthropogenic climate change.*

## Conclusion. Thirty Years Later: Bound to Nature in a Digital Society

### The Digital Republic

In 2017, *The New Yorker* published a 7600-word essay by Nathan Heller, entitled "Estonia, the Digital Republic."[208] The article opens in an effusive tone: "Its government is virtual, borderless, blockchained, and secure. Has this

---

[206] Kask, 57.
[207] Uku Alakivi, "Kas jõhvikamarjale on vaja korjamistähtaega?," *Eesti Loodus*, no. 8 (1982): 496–97.
[208] Nathan Heller, "Estonia – the Digital Republic," *The New Yorker*, December 11, 2017, www.newyorker.com/magazine/2017/12/18/estonia-the-digital-republic (accessed 15 January, 2020).

tiny post-Soviet nation found the way of the future?"[209] The readers are then regaled with a detailed account of "e-Estonia" which is described as

> the most ambitious project in technological statecraft today, for it includes all members of the government, and alters citizens' daily lives. The normal services that government is involved with – legislation, voting, education, justice, health care, banking, taxes, policing, and so on – have been digitally linked across one platform, wiring up the nation.[210]

The journalist also visits the NATO Cooperative Cyber Defense Centre of Excellence, a think tank and training facility (established in the wake of Russia's 2007 cyberattack on Estonia), the goal of which, we are told, is "to guide other NATO nations toward vigilance."[211] And this is what we hear about the E.U. Digital Summit, held in Tallinn in 2017. Kersti Kaljulaid, the President of Estonia, presents herself as the "President to a digital society" and earns hearty approval from the other leaders of the European states. During her speech, Emmanuel Macron is reported as "nodding vigorously" and Angela Merkel is deeply impressed: "You're so much further than we are."[212]

The article ends with the journalist's declaration that what the United States has done wrong, Estonia has done right: "the U.S. had taken one path – personalization, anonymity, information privatization, and competitive efficiency – while Estonia had taken the other" – that of building a digital society.[213] It is also mentioned that Skype was developed in Estonia and that Estonia supports a flourishing start-up culture. Estonians, the reader understands, feel that their task is to enlighten and lead the rest of Europe and its allies in NATO.

Heller's article was hardly an exception: many appearances of Estonia in the Western press during the 2010s had to do with Estonia's digital achievements.[214] Such press reports, frequently relayed back in Estonian newspapers and social media, contributed to Estonians' shared sense of living in a developed, digitally

---

[209] Heller.    [210] Heller.    [211] Heller.    [212] Heller.    [213] Heller.

[214] "Welcome to E-stonia, the World's Most Digitally Advanced Society," *Wired*, October 20. 2016, www.wired.co.uk/article/digital-estonia; "Lessons from the Most Digitally Advanced Country in the World," *Forbes*, January 15, 2018, www.forbes.com/sites/peterhigh/2018/01/15/lessons-from-the-most-digitally-advanced-country-in-the-world/#61320da21ac0; Von Reinhold von Eben-Worlée, "Wo Estland Deutschland abhängt," October 11, 2018, www.welt.de/debatte/kommentare/article181941414/Estland-Der-Ruf-als-digitales-Musterland-ist-mehr-als-gerechtfertigt.html; Anaïs Cherif et Pierre Manière, "L'Estonie – royaume du toute tout-numérique," May 4, 2018, www.latribune.fr/technos-medias/internet/l-estonie-royaume-du-tout-numerique-774138.html (all accessed December 8, 2024); Aro Velmet, "The Blank Slate E-State: Estonian Information Society and the Politics of Novelty in the 1990s," *Engaging Science, Technology, and Society* 6 (2020): 162–84.

advanced country. "I think that the E-stonia is really cool (*kihvt*). Kind of brings forward our essence!" reports one interviewee to researcher Kerstin Mahlapuu in 2013.[215]

Yet digital success was just one component of Estonian identity narratives in the 2010s. The other major identificatory cluster was grounded in the sense of belonging together with local environments – with land, soil, forests, and sea.

## Eco-digital Nationhood

The core of the canonized understanding of Estonian identity in the 2010s can be articulated as an eco-digital nationhood. The "eco" part of this conception contains an imaginary link to ancient times: Estonians have, according to this popular narrative, retained an eco-intimacy, an intimate connection with their natural environments. Whereas processes of modernization and technologization broke this ancient bond in other developed nations, Estonians, according to this story, have developed in harmony with forces of nature and have managed to keep their own natural bond intact.

As we have seen in the earlier sections of this Element, many aspects of this narrative flourished as part of Estonian cultural imaginaries during the Soviet era. The early years of independence had seen such visions lose their prominence (and, as we saw in Section 4, there were already some ambiguities the 1970s), yet the 2010s witnessed their re-emergence in powerful new cultural combinations.

According to the eco-digital narrative, Estonians are intimately bound to nature, yet are proud to live in a society on the forefront of the digital frontier. As the bestselling author Valdur Mikita summed it up in 2017, "the true Estonian has Skype in one hand and a small mushroom knife in the other."[216]

There is a paradox embedded in the combination of the ecological and the digital: technological advancements facilitate processes that turn natural environments into spectacle, something that might be comfortably enjoyed from a climate-controlled, pest-free room. Nature photography and nature-documentaries offer cases in point; the fully digital version of eco-intimacy offers the pleasure of enjoying nature on the screen. Indeed, new technologies can produce environmental experiences of an extraordinary kind: in 2018, unexpectedly large audiences – 41,000 people in tiny Estonia – visited movie theatres to see a new documentary about Estonian wildlife, *Tuulte tahutud maa* [*A Wind-Sculpted Land*], directed by Joosep Matjus, a film whose list of characters includes moose, mink, otter, wild pigs, swans, frogs, birds, spiders, fish – and not a single human being (Figure 38).

---

[215] Kerstin Mahlapuu, "Returned to 'Normality'? Estonian National Identity Constructions after EU and NATO Accession. PhD Thesis" (University of Glasgow, 2019), 199.

[216] Valdur Mikita and Rainer Kerge, "Intervjuu: Eesti märk peaks olema 'Igav liiv ja tühi väli'," *Eesti Loodus*, no. 3 (2017): 46.

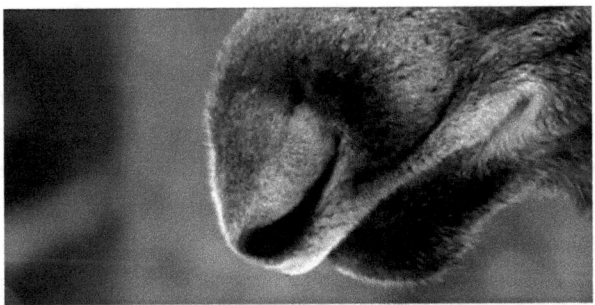

**Figure 38** Still from the film Tuulte tahutud maa [A Wind-Sculpted Land], 2018, directed by Joosep Matjus.

The camera lens created an astonishing digital sense of intimacy: one could, for example, admire a close-up of a moose's ear, eye, or nose, filling the entire screen. The most advanced technology provided viewers with close encounters with non-domesticated living beings, such as would be impossible to realize in the flesh. As the critic Peeter Laurits remarked, "filming nature has nowadays become a highly technical field ... Honestly, I don't know how this team has managed, while encumbered with such colossal technical equipment, to deliver such an intimate sense of nature and make this available for viewers."[217]

Other versions of eco-digital innovation include technologically supported mini gardening within one's homely comfort zone – take, for example, the company Click & Grow, which started on Hiiumaa island but now sells most of its supposedly self-sustaining "smart" indoor gardens on the North American and Asian markets. A 2014 newspaper article declared that these gardens operate on technology that could feed whole cities in the future – an article about their move to Dubai carried the title "Estonian Company Will Create Oases in the Desert."[218]

Watching nature documentaries on the big screen, growing plants in miniature indoor garden beds – all such combinations of technology and nature produce rather ambiguous results. Yet the eco and the digital can also function as two alternating registers or modes of selfhood, to be switched according to one's moods, desires, or possibilities.

## A Twenty-First-Century Estonian Culture of Eco-intimacy

"For of the forest you are, and to the forest you shall return," writes the science journalist Tiit Kändler in 2017, twisting the biblical idiom, but thereby gesturing to the mythical dimensions of forest-related discussions in the Estonian

---
[217] Peeter Laurits, "Kalligraafiline tuul," *Sirp*, September 28, 2018.
[218] Kadri Põlendik, "Eesti firma hakkab kõrbesse oaase rajama," *Äripäev*, December 12, 2014, 10.

public space.[219] In public and social media, one of the dominant manifestations of the eco-narrative in the 2010s was the environmentalist critique of the Estonian state's forestry policy and of forest-cutting in general. Asko Lõhmus's review articles refer to about 120 popular articles written on these topics from late 2016 to August 2019.[220] In the 2010s, the topic of deforestation became one of the central issues discussed in the national media, joined by other environmental topics, such as the ecological implications of the construction of Rail Baltica, a high-speed railway to connect the Baltics with Central Europe. To sum up, in Linda Kaljundi's words from 2018: "If one had to name one keyword that in recent years has most excited public opinion, it might very well be 'environment.'"[221]

The Estonian public space of the 2010s resounded with expressions of care and concern on a range of environmental topics,[222] but the environmental narrative as such was perhaps most fully articulated by the writer Valdur Mikita, who holds a BA in biology and a PhD in semiotics. Collections of Mikita's lyrical essays topped the bestseller lists of the 2010s; the weekly *Eesti Ekspress* designated him a cult writer in 2014.[223] In Mikita's account of Estonian or Finno-Ugric or Baltic Finnic or Nordic particularism, "old Europe" has forsaken its ancient bond between nature and people, whereas Estonians have sustained an intimate relationship with their natural environments.[224] Another essayist, developing this widely shared line of thinking, claims that Estonians have "to some extent retained the indigenous mentality of the Finno-Ugrians," but, as for "the connection with soil, water and forest – you cannot see this much in 'old' Europe anymore."[225] Mikita himself goes further, suggesting that a specific unity of nature, language and culture is found in Estonia: "Estonian particularity consists in its proximity of culture and nature, in its unity of language and nature."[226]

---

[219] Tiit Kändler, "Metsapoole mälestused," *Eesti Loodus*, no. 3 (2017): 30.

[220] Asko Lõhmus, "Mida on näidanud aasta metsapoleemikat," *Sirp*, September 1, 2017; Asko Lõhmus, "Metsapoleemika teine aasta: rägastiku võim," *Sirp*, September 14, 2018; Asko Lõhmus, "Metsapoleemika kolmandal aastal ronisid kollid kapist välja," *Sirp*, August 30, 2019.

[221] Linda Kaljundi, "Uusmetsik Eesti," *Vikerkaar*, no. 7–8 (2018): 68.

[222] The popular critical journal *Vikerkaar*, for example, published two special issues in the late 2010s (no. 7–8, 2018 and 9, 2019) with ecological themes. The 2019 issue was composed of short opinion pieces and included two collectively signed manifestos and texts by about forty writers.

[223] Vahur Afanasjev and Valdur Mikita, "Areeni kaanelugu: Valdur Mikita, metsik isekirjutaja," *Eesti Ekspress*, January 24, 2014.

[224] Valdur Mikita often refers to the Baltic Finnic subgroup of Finno-Ugrians as his point of reference – Finns, Karelians, Veps, and a few other living ethnic groups are included in the same set.

[225] Kaido Kama, "Eurooplate vastutus," *Vikerkaar*, no. 9 (2019): 126.

[226] Valdur Mikita, *Lingvistiline mets: tsibihärblase paradigma. Teadvuse kiirendi* (Tallinn: Grenader, 2013), 142.

Valdur Mikita foregrounds local or Baltic Finnic traditions as unique and as related to the still existing deep forestation of these areas.[227] His popularity stemmed from his masterful attunement, amplification, and development of already-existing currents of thought in the 2010s. His eco-narrative is partly also an eco-digital narrative; Mikita argues for a necessary balance between Europeanness and local Baltic-Finnic traditions. For example, he emphasizes the ability of Estonians to switch from the "eco"-register to the digital world: in his semi-mythological vision, an Estonian man digs his garden on Mondays and mines his bitcoins on Tuesdays and knows both how to code and how to shoe a horse.[228]

## Blind Spots in the Eco-digital Vision

Like any frame of vision, the eco-digital narrative is selective in what it sees and what it considers. The European Commission Country Reports, for example, judge Estonia as suffering many symptoms of concern: income inequality is relatively high, poverty risks for the elderly and the unemployed are high, and the social safety net is inadequate in important respects.[229] One report summarizes its findings: "Relatively low spending on social protection and the limited capacity of the tax and benefit system to redistribute wealth may explain the high income inequality."[230] The gender pay-gap is reported as high and productivity growth as weak. Self-reported unmet need for medical care is among the highest in the EU, due to long wait times.[231] Nor was Estonia on track to create a recycling economy. Local inhabitants could have listed many additional social problems in need of remedy, some inherited from the Soviet era, some related to post-Soviet neoliberal policies, some reflecting transnational trends: the accumulation of capital and population in the capital city of Tallinn, shortages of doctors, teachers, and highly skilled workers, the persistence of racial prejudice.

Estonia's dominant, eco-digital national imaginary of the 2010s was produced by an aesthetic screening, supported by a Western gaze, and adapted for local purposes of positive identity-creation. In this screening process, dissonant

---

[227] Kaljundi, "Uusmetsik Eesti," 70. For Kaljundi's critique of Mikita's views, see also Linda Kaljundi, "Eestlus – loodusrahvamüüt keskkonnakriisi ajastul," *Vikerkaar*, no. 9 (2019): 114–18.

[228] Valdur Mikita, *Kukeseene kuulamise kunst. Läänemeresoome elutunnet otsimas* (Vara: Välgi metsad, 2017), 42.

[229] European Commission, "Country Report Estonia 2018" (Brussels, 2018), 20, 21. See also Aet Annist's research about processes of individualization and the collapse of village society in the post-Soviet years: Aet Annist, *Otsides kogukonda sotsialismijärgses keskuskülas. Arenguantropoloogiline uurimus* (Tallinn: Tallinn University Press, 2011).

[230] European Commission, "Country Report Estonia 2018," 6. See also European Commission, *Country Report Estonia 2019* (Brussels, 2019), 17.

[231] European Commission, *2023 Country Report: Estonia* (Luxembourg: Publications Office of the European Union, 2023).

aspects of the past – for example, complications of its Soviet heritage, whether material, demographic, social, or psychological – were simply omitted.

## Conclusion: From the End of the Soviet Union to the 2020s

Estonia's cultural changes following the collapse of the Soviet Union can be conceptualized as moving from decolonization toward eco-digital nationhood. In the 1980s, the popular mood among Estonian-speakers included anxiety over the national future under what was commonly understood as "Russian rule," with its heavy Russophone immigration and the deepening penetration of Russian language use into different social spheres. In reaction, by the late 1980s and early 1990s, the prevailing popular sentiment might be broadly described as one of decolonization. By the 2010s, decolonization had run its course, prevailing public moods and imaginaries had shifted significantly, and the dominant eco-digital discourse focused on present national success rather than on lingering effects of the Soviet past. The contrast with the 1990s is striking: if, in the 1990s, Soviet-era military bases (to pick one example) carried a strongly negative affective weight as signifiers of colonial oppression, by the 2010s, their emotional charge had dissipated and these sites found new life as cultural heritage sites (Figure 39). Some of them became protected under the Heritage Conservation Act, and efforts were made to document, restore, and conserve amateur art from the military bases.[232] It is especially noteworthy that according to the project leader Hilkka Hiiop, public comment on this work in social media and in newspaper commentary was largely positive, thus indicating a general support for such projects.[233]

The early 2020s have once again imposed a crisis mode upon Estonian (and global) identities and politics. The coronavirus pandemic since January 2020, the renewal of Russia's imperial aggression, the intensification, since February 2022, of Russia's war against Ukraine, the devastation of climate change – once more, global and regional processes have asserted their imperatives over the local and the national. Estonia's political gains of the 2000s, joining the European Union and NATO, have now emerged as its best assurance for the survival of the state and the nation. The European Union has helped support governmental efforts to move more decisively toward sustainable practices, while NATO membership has provided the only credible guarantee against a new Russian annexation.

---

[232] "Soviet Mural Enjoys Rare Estonian Restoration," *Bbc.com*, September 28, 2017, www.bbc.com/news/blogs-news-from-elsewhere-41427733 (accessed 8 December, 2024). Robert Treufeldt and Hilkka Hiiop, "Difficult Stories of a Difficult Legacy: Researches, Problems and Solutions in Conserving Art from within the Soviet Armed Forces" (paper presented at the symposium The Soviet Otherwise: Affects, Margins, and Imaginaries, Kurtna, Estonia, July 25–26, 2019).

[233] Treufeldt and Hiiop.

**Figure 39** Restoring a mural at the naval base on Naissaare Island, Estonia. Photo: The Estonian Academy of Arts.

As for environmental thought, the COVID-era surge in gardening and trends in counter-urbanization have shaved off some of the ambiguity from Estonians' eco-digital imaginaries. Click-and-Grow indoor mini-gardens have been set aside by tending to actual gardens, an activity promoted globally for its stress-reducing qualities, and through the growing emphasis on sustainable practices. As for imaginaries of nationhood, eco-digital or otherwise, the sense of a nation facing a range of crises casts a gloomy shadow over any effort to provide positive models for identity-building.

And yet, in the traditional presidential address delivered in the minutes before the New Year, on December 31, 2023, the Estonian president Alar Karis started and ended his speech with verses written by Paul-Eerik Rummo in the 1960s. Rummo's hymnic poem is structured around the central image of a "family of bees," and it depicts the struggle of facing the stormy sea. In President Karis's speech, the calls for unity in civic nationalism were expressed through the image of bumble bees, and the political challenges had taken the shape of a stormy sea – thus providing us with a reassurance that romantic imaginaries of nature, tested through years of Soviet rule, continue to play a suggestive role in Estonians' political and cultural self-conception.

# Acknowledgments

This research was supported by grants "Patterns of Development in Estonian Culture of the Transition Period," (PRG636) and "Memory and Environment: The Intersection of Fast and Slow Violence in Transnational European Literature" (PRG2592), both from the Estonian Ministry of Education and Research, and "Strengthening of the professional competences of the academic staff in strategic specialization areas in Daugavpils University, 3rd round" No 8.2.2.0/20/I/003. Section 1 includes material from Epp Annus, "Rethinking Soviet Selfhood in the Era of the Anthropocene: From the Foucauldian Paradigm to the Naturecultural Theory of the Subject," Slavic Review 82.2 (2023). The epilogue uses material from Epp Annus, "A Post-Soviet Eco-Digital Nation? Metonymic Processes of Nation-Building and Estonia's High-Tech Dreams in the 2010s," East European Politics and Societies 36.2 (2022). Robert Hughes was of invaluable assistance in the initial editing of the manuscript. I thank the reviewers and the editors of this Element.

I also thank my friends and colleagues Virve Sarapik and Piret Viires for their invaluable support on many fronts. Our longstanding *Nüüdiskultuuri uurimise* research group, with its intense discussions, congenial atmosphere, and commitment to bringing together detailed knowledge with critical analysis, is surely the best in the world – I am grateful to Virve for keeping us together. I also thank Linda Kaljundi for our thoughtful discussions, and many other scholars whose work has paved the ground for this research. I am also deeply grateful to all those people – tens of thousands – who cared about the environment during the period of my research. And as always, suur aitäh Robbekaasa!

Cambridge Elements =

# Soviet and Post-Soviet History

## Mark Edele
*University of Melbourne*

Mark Edele teaches Soviet history at the University of Melbourne, where he is Hansen Professor in History. His most recent books are *Stalinism at War* (2021) *and Russia's War Against Ukraine* (2023). He is one of the convenors of the Research Initiative on Post-Soviet Space (RIPSS) at the University of Melbourne.

## Rebecca Friedman
*Florida International University*

Rebecca Friedman is Founding Director of the Wolfsonian Public Humanities Lab and Professor of History at Florida International University in Miami. Her recent book, Modernity, Domesticity and Temporality: Time at Home, supported by the National Endowment for the Humanities, explores modern time and home in twentieth century Russia (2020). She is one of the editors for the Bloomsbury Academic series A Cultural History of Time.

### About the Series

Elements in Soviet and Post-Soviet History pluralise the history of the former Soviet space. Contributions decolonise Soviet history and provincialise the former metropole: Russia. In doing so, the series provides an up-to-date history of the present of the region formerly known as the Soviet Union.

# Cambridge Elements

## Soviet and Post-Soviet History

### Elements in the Series

*Making National Diasporas:*
*Soviet-Era Migrations and Post-Soviet Consequences*
Lewis H. Siegelbaum and Leslie Page Moch

*Ukraine not 'the' Ukraine*
Marta Dyczok

*The Fate of the Soviet Bloc's Military Alliance:*
*Reform, Adaptation, and Collapse of the Warsaw Pact, 1985–1991*
Mark Kramer

*Central Asia – Russia's Near Abroad or Crossroads of Asia?*
Richard Pomfret

*Decolonizing Russia?: Disentangling Debates*
Adam Lenton et al.

*Environment and Society in Soviet Estonia, 1960–1990:*
*An Intimate Cultural History*
Epp Annus

A full series listing is available at: www.cambridge.org/ESPH

For EU product safety concerns, contact us at Calle de José Abascal, 56–1°, 28003 Madrid, Spain or eugpsr@cambridge.org.

www.ingramcontent.com/pod-product-compliance
Lightning Source LLC
LaVergne TN
LVHW020349260326
834688LV00045B/1627